Management of Risk:
Guidance for Practitioners

London : TSO

Published by TSO (The Stationery Office) and available from:

Online
www.tsoshop.co.uk

Mail, Telephone, Fax & E-mail
TSO
PO Box 29, Norwich, NR3 1GN
Telephone orders/General enquiries: 0870 600 5522
Fax orders: 0870 600 5533
E-mail: customer.services@tso.co.uk
Textphone 0870 240 3701

TSO Shops
16 Arthur Street, Belfast BT1 4GD
028 9023 8451 Fax 028 9023 5401
71 Lothian Road, Edinburgh EH3 9AZ
0870 606 5566 Fax 0870 606 5588

TSO@Blackwell and other Accredited Agents

Published for the Office of Government Commerce under licence from the Controller of Her Majesty's Stationery Office.

First Edition Crown copyright 2002
Second Edition Crown copyright 2007

First published 2007

Second impression with corrections 2007

ISBN 978 0 11 331038 8

Printed in the United Kingdom for The Stationery Office
N 5615595   c30   08/07

Contents

Foreword

All of us manage risks in our daily lives almost unconsciously – assessing the speed of traffic when crossing the road, taking out insurance policies, making everyday decisions, weighing up options. However, in business, risk and risk management can sometimes be seen as specialist subjects, requiring expertise outside 'normal' management experience. In other circumstances, risk can be ignored altogether or the view taken that risk can be avoided by maintaining the status quo. Spending time developing risk management strategies is sometimes perceived as mere pointless bureaucracy.

In this rapidly changing world, a status quo is unrealistic, and failure to identify and explore new opportunities is a risk in itself. The difference between a thriving, growing business and stagnation could be the willingness to embrace a risk taking culture that allows your organisation to develop opportunities for innovation while taking timely and appropriate action in the face of threats to achieving your business objectives.

This guide provides an accessible framework for taking informed decisions on managing risk throughout the organisation, from designing policy and strategy to dealing with threats and opportunities in your day-to-day operations and services. M_o_R is designed to provide you, as a manager, with the tools you need to meet all your business objectives, to improve service delivery to your customers and achieve real value for money.

Peter Fanning
Deputy Chief Executive Officer
Office of Government Commerce

Acknowledgements

Authoring Team

John Bartlett   Adviza Consultants Ltd
Robert Chapman   Siemens Insight Consulting
Andrew Schuster   Independent Consultant
Graham Williams   GSW Consultancy

In order to maintain M_o_R's reflection of current best practice and to produce guidance with lasting value, OGC consulted widely with key stakeholders at every stage in the process. OGC would like to thank the following individuals and their organisations for their contributions to refreshing the M_o_R guidance.

Reference Group

Peter Campbell   APM Risk SIG
Steve Daniels   Siemens Insight Consulting
Nicky Dennis   British Standards Institute (BSI)
Michael Faber   Institute of Operational Risk/
                     JP Morgan Cazenove
Edmund Hughes   HM Treasury
Michael Ocock   Institute of Risk Management
Frances Scarff   OGC
Brian Toft   Coventry University and Risk
                     Partnerships
Colin Wheeler   Istria Ltd

A number of people generously contributed their time and expertise to ensuring the quality of this publication. Anne-Marie Byrne, as OGC Project Executive, is grateful for the additional support provided by Zoe Peden to the authoring team on the development of this book and particular thanks go to Siemens Insight Consulting for their continuing support of M_o_R. The following individuals provided additional quality assurance as members of the Change Control Panel – Mike Pears, Andrew Wood and John Humphries.

Reviewers

Carol Bartlett   Amicar Consulting
John Bartlett   Great Stave
John Bell   OGC
Chris Churchouse   Best Practice User Group (BPUG)
Peter Clark   OGC
Rubina Faber   Regal Training
Alan Ferguson   AFA
Michael Hardie   Stoke on Trent County Council
Jo Howey   HM Treasury
Val Jonas   Risk Decisions Group
Tony Levene   Quality Projects (Consulting) Limited
Stephen Marks   Project Performance Consulting Ltd
Tim Reeks   HM Revenue & Customs
Alan Summerfield   Aspire Europe
Mike Ward   Outperform UK Ltd

Introduction

1 Introduction

1.1 PURPOSE OF THIS GUIDE

This guide is intended to help organisations put in place an effective framework for taking informed decisions about the risks that affect their performance objectives across all organisational activities, whether these be strategic, programme, project or operational.

It provides a route map for risk management, bringing together principles, an approach, a set of inter-related processes and pointers to more detailed sources of advice on risk management techniques and specialisms. It also provides advice on how these principles, approach and processes should be embedded, reviewed and applied differently depending on the nature of the objectives at risk.

The M_o_R framework is based on four core concepts as shown in Figure 1.1.

Figure 1.1 M_o_R framework

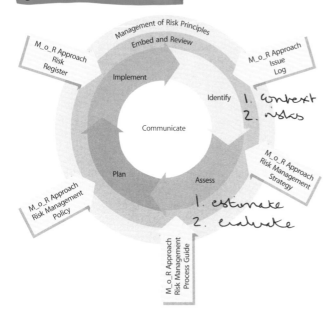

1. context
2. risks

1. estimate
2. evaluate

- **M_o_R principles**. These principles are essential for the development of good risk management practice. They are all derived from corporate governance principles in the recognition that risk management is a subset of any organisation's internal controls.
- **M_o_R approach**. These principles need to be adapted and adopted to suit each individual organisation. Accordingly, an organisation's approach to these principles needs to be agreed and defined

within a Risk Management Policy, Process Guide and Strategies, and be supported by the use of Risk Registers and Issue Logs.

- **M_o_R processes**. These four main process steps describe the inputs, outputs and activities involved in ensuring that risks are identified, assessed and controlled.
- **Embedding and reviewing M_o_R.** Having put in place these principles, approach and processes, an organisation needs to ensure that they are consistently applied across the organisation and that their application undergoes continual improvement in order for them to be effective.

1.2 WHAT IS RISK?

In this guide **'risk'** is defined as 'an uncertain event or set of events which, should it occur, will have an effect on the achievement of objectives'. A risk consists of a combination of the probability of a perceived threat or opportunity occurring and the magnitude of its impact on objectives. Within this definition 'threat' is used to describe an uncertain event that could have a negative impact on objectives or benefits; and 'opportunity' is used to describe an uncertain event that could have a favourable impact on objectives or benefits.

1.3 WHAT IS RISK MANAGEMENT?

Every organisation manages its risk, but not always in a way that is visible, repeatable or consistent, to support effective decision-making. The task of risk management is to ensure that an organisation makes cost-effective use of a risk management process that includes a series of well-defined steps. The aim is to support better decision-making through a good understanding of risks and their likely impact.

Accordingly, the term **'risk management'** refers to the systematic application of principles, approach and processes to the tasks of identifying and assessing risks, and then planning and implementing risk responses. This provides a disciplined environment for proactive decision-making.

For risk management to be effective, risks need to be:

- **Identified.** This includes risks being considered that could affect the achievement of objectives within the context of a particular organisational activity; and then described to ensure that there is a common understanding of these risks.
- **Assessed.** This includes ensuring that each risk can be ranked in terms of estimated impact and immediacy; and understanding the overall level of risk associated with the organisational activity being studied.
- **Controlled.** This includes identifying appropriate responses to risks, assigning owners and then executing, monitoring and controlling these responses.

1.4 WHY IS RISK MANAGEMENT IMPORTANT?

A certain amount of risk taking is inevitable if an organisation is to achieve its objectives. Those organisations that are more risk aware appreciate that actively managing threats and opportunities provides them with a competitive advantage. Taking and managing risk is the very essence of business survival and growth.

Effective risk management is likely to improve performance against objectives by contributing to:

- Better service delivery
- Reduction in management time spent fire-fighting
- Increased likelihood of change initiatives being achieved
- More focus internally on doing the right things properly
- Better basis for strategy setting
- Achievement of competitive advantage
- Fewer sudden shocks and unwelcome surprises
- More efficient use of resources
- Reduced waste and fraud, and better value for money
- Improved innovation
- Better management of contingent and maintenance activities.

Many of these benefits are applicable to both the private and public sectors. Whereas corporations focus mainly on shareholder returns and the preservation of shareholder value, the public sector's role is to implement programmes cost-effectively, in accordance with government legislation and policies to achieve value for money.

In a briefing document produced by the Institute of Chartered Accountants in England and Wales (ICAEW 1999) to aid the implementation of the Turnbull Report (Implementing Turnbull, A Boardroom Briefing, Centre for Business Performance) the benefits of implementing risk management are spelt out as follows:

- A risk-based approach can make a company more flexible and responsive to market fluctuations making it better able to satisfy customers' ever-changing needs in a continually evolving business environment.
- Companies can gain an early-mover advantage by adapting to new circumstances faster than their rivals, which again could lead to competitive advantage in the medium to long term.
- External perceptions of a company are affected by the level of risk that it faces and by the way its risks are managed.
- A major risk exposure and source of business failure and/or lack of opportunity success has been a failure to manage change.
- Companies need to be aware of changing markets, service delivery and morale.
- Effective risk management and internal control can be used to manage change, to all levels of people in the company in meeting its business objectives, and to improve a company's credit rating and ability to raise funds in the future, not to mention its share price over the longer term.

Reproduced from Implementing Turnbull: A Boardroom Briefing, 1999 with permission The Institute of Chartered Accountants in England and Wales.

1.5 RECENT DEVELOPMENTS IN THE MANAGEMENT OF RISK

Risk management is not a new concept for organisations, as risk has always been an inherent feature in any undertaking. The nature of risk management, however, has evolved rapidly over recent years. It was only in the 1960s that risk management began to be recognised as one of the essential skills required for management. The earliest application of risk management within organisations tended to focus on insurance management in terms of establishing financial capacity for the negative effects of adverse events. During the 1970s a broader view began to emerge whereby organisations began to develop a better understanding of the nature of the risks being faced and looked at alternatives to insurance. There remained, however, a focus on the negative effects of risk.

Only in recent years have organisations begun to recognise that risk management, in its broadest sense, can be applied to both negative threats and positive opportunities. In each case a proactive approach is required that seeks to reduce the size of the possible threat or increase that of the possible opportunity. Whilst it may be tempting to consider these as separate activities, in practice opportunities and threats are seldom independent.

The first edition of this guide was published in 2002 in response to the Turnbull Report to provide a generic framework for risk management across all parts of an organisation. Since then the world of risk management has moved forward:

- In the UK public sector HM Treasury has revised its Orange Book (outlining the principles and concepts of risk management) and its Green Book (providing a best practice guide for the appraisal and evaluation of government initiatives), and various additional reports have been issued such as:
  - Guidance on Internal Control and Risk Management in Principal Local Authorities and other Relevant Bodies to Support Compliance with the Accounts and Audit Regulations (CIPFA 2003)
  - Managing Risks to Improve Public Services (National Audit Office 2004).
- In the private sector change has been instigated in the UK, across Europe and within the US by new regulatory environments driven for instance by the:
  - Combined Code on Corporate Governance 2006 (UK)
  - Basel II Accord 2004 (Bank of International Settlements, Switzerland)
  - Sarbanes-Oxley 2002 (Public Company Accounting Reform and Investor Protection Act, US).

Whilst this guide has been produced in the UK and has primary examples based on UK regulations, it has been designed to be of benefit to both domestic and international organisations.

1.6 CORPORATE GOVERNANCE AND INTERNAL CONTROL

A major factor influencing the drive towards more formalised approaches to risk management has been the increased focus given to corporate governance in both the UK and the US following the high-profile collapses of companies such as the Bank of Credit and Commerce International (BCCI), the Maxwell Communication Corporation plc (MCC), Enron and WorldCom.

Corporate governance can be defined as the ongoing activity of maintaining a sound system of internal control by which the directors and officers of an organisation ensure that effective management systems, including financial monitoring and control systems, have been put

in place to protect assets, earnings capacity and the reputation of the organisation. It covers a wide range of topics, including directors' remuneration; accountability and audit; relations with shareholders; and relations with institutional shareholders.

In the UK since 1992 various reports and an evolutionary sequence of Combined Codes from the Financial Services Authority (FSA) have pushed organisations to continually improve their internal controls and risk management. The essential elements of the Combined Code on Corporate Governance (last revised in 2006) that have influenced M_o_R's principles are summarised by the following questions:

- Can non-executive directors satisfy themselves that financial information is accurate and that financial controls and systems of risk management are robust and defensible?
- Does the audit committee carry out reviews of the company's internal financial control system and, unless expressly addressed by a separate risk committee or by the board itself, its risk management systems?
- Does the board have clear strategies for dealing with the significant risks that have been identified and is there a policy on how to manage these risks?
- Do the company's culture, code of conduct, human resource policies and performance reward systems support the business objectives and the risk management and internal control system?
- Do people in the company (and in its outsourced services) have the knowledge, skills and tools to support the achievement of the company's objectives and to manage effectively risks to their achievement?

In the US a more radical approach was taken resulting in new legislation in the form of the Public Company Accounting Reform and Investor Protection Act of 2002 (also known as Sarbanes-Oxley). The main thrust of the Act is to influence the behaviour and conduct of public companies to ensure that they issue informative and accurate financial statements. Of particular note in the context of risk management are the following provisions:

- The Chief Executive Officer (CEO) and the Chief Financial Officer (CFO) of public companies are held personally accountable for establishing and maintaining internal controls and evaluating their effectiveness. They are also responsible for advising their auditors of all significant deficiencies in the design or operation of the internal controls.
- Public companies are required to include in each annual report an internal control report that states the responsibility of management to establish and

maintain an adequate internal control structure and procedures for financial reporting and an assessment of the effectiveness of these.

Sarbanes-Oxley is more onerous than the UK's Combined Code 2006 as it requires the organisation's management to report on the effectiveness of its internal controls and auditors to report on the assessment made by management.

For those organisations operating in the financial services industry, Basel II is of particular note. This report was issued in 2004 and is a revision of the original framework. Its aim was to make the framework more risk sensitive and representative of modern banks' risk management practices. The original Basel Accord (Basel I) was agreed in 1988 and contains capital requirement rules stating that credit

institutions, such as banks and building societies, must at all times maintain a minimum amount of financial capital in order to cover the risks to which they are exposed. The aim is to ensure the financial soundness of such institutions, to maintain customer confidence in the solvency of the institutions, to ensure the stability of the financial system at large, and to protect depositors against losses.

1.7 INTERNAL CONTROL AND RISK MANAGEMENT

In the same way that internal control is one aspect of corporate governance, risk management is one aspect of internal control (alongside financial, operational and

Figure 1.2 Composition of the Combined Code 2006 and its relationship to the Turnbull guidance

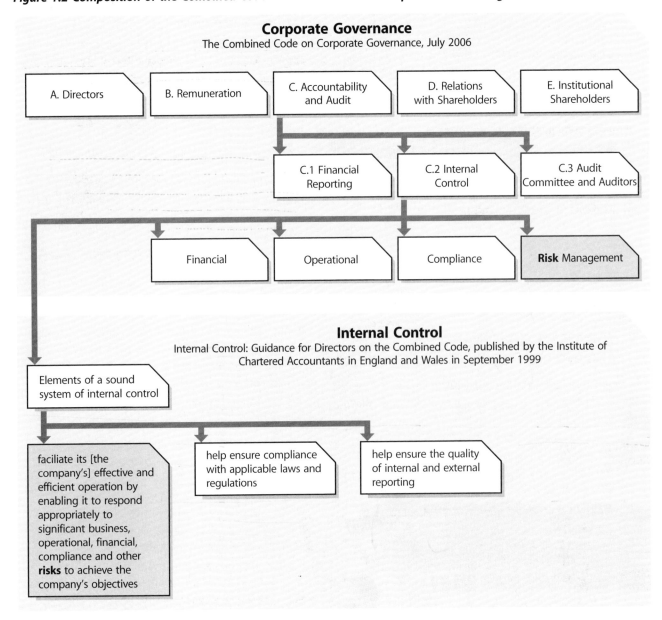

Corp. ga →
internal controls
(fin) (op) (info) (comp)

compliance). The revised guidance for directors on the Combined Code states that:

> A company's system of internal control has a key role in the management of risks that are significant to the fulfilment of its business objectives. A sound system of internal control contributes to safeguarding the shareholders' investment and the company assets.

The Combined Code also states that:

> A company's objectives, its internal organisation and the environment in which it operates are continually evolving, and as a result, the risks it faces are continually changing. A sound system of control therefore depends on a thorough and regular evaluation of the nature and extent of the risks to which the company is exposed. Since profits are in part the reward for successful risk taking in business, the purpose of internal control is to help manage and control risk rather than to eliminate it.

Figure 1.2 illustrates the relationship of corporate governance to internal control and to risk management.

1.8 WHERE AND WHEN SHOULD RISK MANAGEMENT BE APPLIED?

Risk management should be most rigorously applied where critical decisions are being made. Decisions about risk will vary depending on whether the risk relates to long-, medium- or short-term goals.

- **Strategic** decisions are primarily concerned with long-term goals; these set the context for decisions at other levels of the organisation. The risks associated with strategic decisions may not become apparent until well into the future. Thus it is essential to review these decisions and associated risks on a regular basis.
- Medium-term goals are usually addressed through **programmes** and **projects** to bring about business change. Decisions relating to medium-term goals are narrower in scope than strategic ones, particularly in terms of timeframe and financial responsibilities.
- At the **operational** level the emphasis is on short-term goals to ensure ongoing continuity of business services; however, decisions about risk at this level must also support the achievement of long- and medium-term goals.

These four organisational perspectives are discussed in more detail in Chapter 6.

Risk management should be applied during decision-making when planning the introduction of change at any of the organisational perspectives referred to above.

1.9 OGC BEST PRACTICE GUIDANCE

1.9.1 Managing Successful Programmes

Managing Successful Programmes (MSP) provides a framework to enable the achievement of high-quality change outcomes and benefits that fundamentally affect the way that organisations work. A key theme within MSP

Figure 1.3 Organisational perspectives

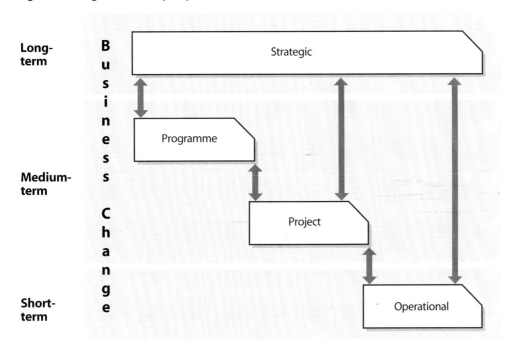

is managing risks to the achievement of a programme's objectives. A programme approach to implementing M_o_R's principles, approach and processes will ensure an organisation is in the best position to maximise the benefits of successful adoption and embedding.

1.9.2 Managing Successful Projects with PRINCE2

PRINCE2 is a structured method to help effective project management. One of the key components of PRINCE2 is management of risk, in recognition that 'project management must control and contain risk if a project is to stand a chance of being successful'. A range of projects may need to be run as part of an organisation's programme for adopting the M_o_R framework.

1.9.3 IT Infrastructure Library

Where the operational environment includes technology, the OGC IT Infrastructure Library (ITIL) is internationally recognised guidance for IT service management that provides a very powerful base for understanding the business-as-usual processes and services at risk.

1.10 HOW TO USE THIS GUIDE

It is recommended that all readers familiarise themselves with the first four chapters of this book, as these provide comprehensive guidance on the most important aspects of risk management. Chapter 5 will be of interest to those with responsibility for reviewing and improving risk management within their organisations and the final chapter will be of interest to those who manage risks within one or more of the four perspectives covered.

Chapter 1 introduces some key terminology and explains what risk management is; why it is important to organisations; and where and when it should be applied. It also provides an introduction to the subjects of corporate governance and internal control.

Chapter 2 outlines the management of risk principles underlying effective risk management in an organisation. These principles are derived from corporate governance and recognise that risk management is a subset of an organisation's internal controls.

Chapter 3 presents the management of risk approach, which consists of the Risk Management Policy, Process Guide, Strategy and Risk Register. It explains the main risk management concepts that need to be considered in establishing these documents.

Chapter 4 describes the main steps of the management of risk process. It contains practical pointers for identifying, assessing, and controlling risks.

Chapter 5 describes and provides guidance on how an organisation can introduce and embed risk management, and then measure the success and maturity of its risk management.

Chapter 6 explains when and how management of risk principles, concepts and processes should be applied throughout an organisation, from the strategic, programme, project and operational perspectives.

The appendices provide supporting detail as follows:

- **A** Management of risk document outlines
  To be read in conjunction with Chapter 3, Management of risk approach

- **B** Common techniques
  To be read in conjunction with Chapter 4, Management of risk process

- **C** Management of risk healthcheck
  To be read in conjunction with Chapter 5, Embedding and reviewing management of risk

- **D** Management of risk maturity model
  To be read in conjunction with Chapter 5, Embedding and reviewing management of risk

- **E** Risk specialisms
  To be read by those with a responsibility for any of the specialisms covered

- **F** Selecting risk management software tools
  To be read by those with responsibility for acquiring software tools to support risk management.

Management of
risk principles

2

2 Management of risk principles

2.1 INTRODUCTION

This chapter describes the management of risk principles. The principles described here are intended to be high-level, universally applicable guidelines for aiding and influencing risk management practices. The 12 principles identified are:

- Organisational context
- Stakeholder involvement
- Organisational objectives
- M_o_R approach
- Reporting
- Roles and responsibilities
- Support structure
- Early warning indicators
- Review cycle
- Overcoming barriers to M_o_R
- Supportive culture
- Continual improvement.

M_o_R principles are essential for the development of good risk management practice. They are intended to be concise, readily understood and easily applicable. They are all derived from proven corporate governance principles in the recognition that risk management is a subset of any organisation's internal controls. These principles are not intended to be prescriptive but provide supportive guidance to enable organisations to develop their own policies, processes, strategies and plans to meet their specific needs.

These principles are evolutionary in nature in that the way they are applied may need to change over time to reflect a change in circumstances. Organisations must innovate and adapt their risk management practices to remain competitive in a changing and uncertain world, so that they can respond to new demands and maximise new opportunities. Additionally, adopted risk management principles must support scalable risk management practices to reflect an organisation's size and the extent of its operations and services. Collectively the principles are aimed at providing a foundation for effective risk

Figure 2.1 Possible sequence of the implementation of M_o_R principles

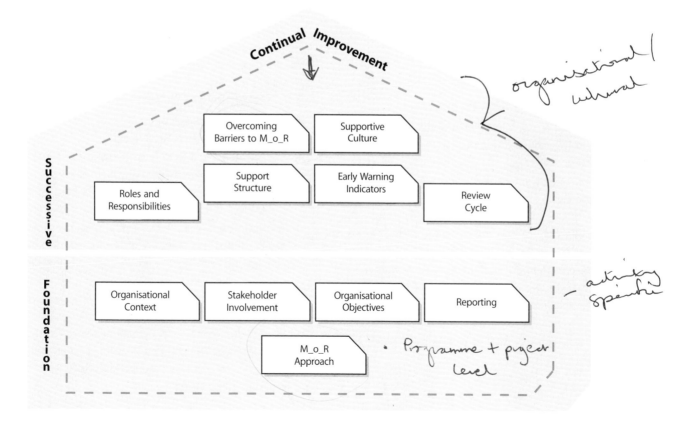

management that contributes to the improvement of organisational performance.

The principles are interdependent and cannot all be implemented simultaneously, i.e. some principles have to be in place before the remainder can be established. The level of benefits derived from a principle will depend on whether it is a 'foundation' principle or whether it is a 'successive' principle. Figure 2.1 describes one possible sequence in which the principles may be implemented. Those principles established first have the greatest initial benefit. Successive principles provide significant benefits, but on a diminishing scale. The sequence in which any one organisation adopts the principles will depend on how long it has been established, its size, organisational structure, management culture and current risk maturity.

2.2 ORGANISATIONAL CONTEXT

A key step of risk management is the identification of threats, opportunities and other areas of uncertainty. Effective identification of these is dependent on an understanding of the context of the organisation or activity under examination to avoid 'blind spots' and subsequent unpleasant surprises. Risk management should reflect the context of the organisation and the activity under examination. The context includes the political, economic, social, technological, legal and environmental backdrop, but also commonly includes the industry, markets, locations, technologies and regulatory regime in which the organisation operates. However, while risk management must take cognisance of the current context, it must also consider how that context may change over time.

2.2.1 Supporting factors

- The context is a primary source of risk – the more complex the context (potentially), the greater the exposure.
- Risk management for the private sector should reflect the context in terms of the authority of other external organisations to impose policies, pricing restrictions, fines, penalties, prohibition notices and closure orders, or order the cessation or suspension of trading.
- Risk management for the public sector should reflect the context more in terms of the disparate subjects of, for example, policies, politics, the national and global economy, technological change, European legislation, demographics, climate change and the budget.

- Organisations should have the ability and capacity of responding quickly to evolving risks to the business arising from factors within the organisation (internal) and to changes in the business environment (external).
- The risk manager must be familiar with the context to be able to ask informed questions and constructively challenge the risks identified and their assessment.
- The risk manager must make explicit the objectives of the organisational activity under examination as risks and opportunities are identified against them.
- The capacity for an organisation to understand both its immediate threats and opportunities and those that are on the horizon (and slowly gaining in clarity) is a measure of its ability to compete.
- The context will influence an organisation's risk appetite, as a result of competitor behaviour, a change in market size, economic pressures, the rate of technological change and interest rate fluctuations.

2.3 STAKEHOLDER INVOLVEMENT

As the trend for increasingly complex, large and costly organisational activities continues unabated, so does the effort required for the management of stakeholders. Large public sector programmes and projects in particular have a vast number of primary stakeholders who are typically a combination of the ultimate end-users plus organisations that are providing funding, approval, scope definition, guidance, design, information, management and financial advice. The lack of timely engagement of these primary stakeholders can be detrimental to establishing, agreeing and achieving an activity's objectives. Risk management should, therefore, involve all primary stakeholders.

2.3.1 Supporting factors

- All major stakeholders of an organisational activity need to be identified and engaged.
- Stakeholders need to be provided with timely, specific and clear information when any new major activity is proposed – detailing what its impact will be on them – throughout the life of the activity.
- The sponsoring stakeholder's main objectives for an activity should be captured, disseminated, discussed, aligned and agreed, with any omissions being signed off.
- Failure to identify and involve all major stakeholders during the identification of the objectives may lead to incomplete objectives or objections to an activity late in its lifecycle. The late introduction of additional objectives can cause a pre-agreed budget and schedule to be exceeded.

- Proactive and early involvement of stakeholders engenders support, acceptance and collective ownership.
- Where appropriate, stakeholders should be included in the identification and assessment of risk.
- Depending on the activity type, stakeholders may have to take responsibility for risk events that materialise.
- It is important to manage stakeholder expectations so that unrealistic objectives are avoided.

2.4 ORGANISATIONAL OBJECTIVES

The success of any organisation is measured by whether it accomplishes its objectives and also whether they are achieved in a satisfactory and responsible way. As the purpose of risk management is to strive to understand and manage the threats to and opportunities arising from these objectives, risk management can only commence when it is clear what these objectives are. In simple terms, risks should be identified against organisational objectives. However, as these objectives are continually evolving, evaluation of the exposure to risk should be conducted on a regular basis.

2.4.1 Supporting factors

- The purpose of risk management is to support an organisation in the securing of its objectives and, hence, necessitates acquiring knowledge about an organisation's objectives.
- Risk identification should not be commenced until the objectives of the organisational activity under examination are clearly understood, captured and disseminated. Where these objectives are not already SMART (specific, measurable, achievable, relevant and time-bound), time must be taken to ensure, as far as possible, that they are SMART.
- When objectives are changed during an activity, the previously identified threats and opportunities (and all of their associated details) should be reviewed and updated.

2.5 M_o_R APPROACH

Organisations should develop an approach to the management of risk that reflects their unique objectives. It is common for organisations to describe their approach through their policies, processes, strategies and plans. Collectively these documents describe the what, when, where, who, how and why. They set out how risks will be identified, assessed and controlled. They indicate when risk management will be carried out, by whom, and for what purpose. They describe risk tolerance levels, escalation rules, methods for calculating contingencies and the approach to be adopted for insurance and reporting cycles. They describe what should be examined. They reflect the context of the organisation and describe the reports to be produced to satisfy governance, shareholders and the regulatory regime, where one exists.

2.5.1 Supporting factors

- The policies, processes, strategies and plans should describe which activities should be routinely subject to risk identification, assessment and control; when during the activities the process should be carried out; who will undertake the risk management steps; who will oversee the application of risk management; and the benefits that the process aims to achieve.
- Risk management policies should reflect the nature and extent of the risks facing the organisation and specifically make explicit the organisation's risk appetite and capacity, in order to aid decision-making (where capacity is an organisation's ability to absorb risk).
- Policies and strategies should be established for the different activities of the organisation to reflect the different types of risk faced.
- Processes should be supported by appropriate tools and techniques that enhance the effectiveness of risk management.
- Risks should be assessed in a way that enables risk management action to be prioritised and to be as effective as possible.
- Escalation procedures should be agreed. This means that if a risk is assessed as having a potential impact exceeding a predetermined authority threshold or if the risk cannot be managed at this level as it relates to senior management activities, it is automatically escalated (by way of pre-agreed channels) to more senior management for decision-making.
- Successful risk taking should be a combination of the maximisation of opportunities and mitigation of threats associated with those opportunities.
- There is no 'one-size-fits-all' risk management solution and so policies, processes and strategies should be tailored to suit the circumstances. Standardised 'tick box' forms alone will leave organisations bereft of an adequate approach and highly exposed.
- The selected approach should be adopted for all processes and reporting to ensure the adoption of best practices and ease of amalgamating information.
- Risk management should be integrated with other disciplines when implemented, to support improvements in programme and project management and other business processes.

2.6 REPORTING

The governing body of organisations should receive, review and act on risk management reports. As a result, a fundamental aspect of risk management is the timely communication of risk information to the management team to enable it to make informed decisions. All significant planned organisational activities should be accompanied by a risk report. It is important for the board of any organisation to receive risk management reports on activities such as acquisitions, divestments, investments, contracts and outsourcing, as well as business as usual. The benefit a board will derive from reports will depend on the quality of the reports; who they were prepared and reviewed by; the interval between the preparation of the report and its receipt; and the window of opportunity to make any form of response.

2.6.1 Supporting factors

- Information needs to be shared with the board or management so that it can respond.
- Informed members of the board should review the reports promptly.
- The reports should be succinct, accurate and focused and include an executive summary for speed of assimilation.
- The reports should make clear the interdependencies between activities and the corresponding risk profile.
- The reports should make clear recommendations.
- Actions that require prompt responses should be highlighted or opportunities will be lost or the chance to reduce an impact will be diminished.
- Where appropriate, reports should include graphical representations of the 'headlines' of the information contained in the report (such as dashboards) to enable senior management or the board to assimilate very quickly the most significant aspects of the report, including trends. Trend analysis will illustrate whether a position is improving or deteriorating.

2.7 ROLES AND RESPONSIBILITIES

When any board establishes the roles to be performed (and the organisational structure to enable those roles to function and deliver the organisational objectives), it has to decide on the commitment it is going to make to risk management. For risk management to be fully supported, there must be an understanding of the need for a risk management role and the responsibilities of that role. As a consequence, the board is instrumental in providing leadership and direction for risk management. A focal point (centre of excellence) and a dedicated resource are

prerequisite for the successful delivery of risk management aims. Risk management must be supported and undertaken by a group that collectively identifies, assesses and controls the risks facing the organisation. This group must fully understand the processes to follow, the escalation rules, reporting requirements, the overall aims of risk management and how success will be measured. In summary, organisations should establish clear roles and responsibilities for the management of risk in terms of leadership, direction, controls, ongoing risk management, reporting and reviewing.

2.7.1 Supporting factors

- For risk management to be effective it must have support and sponsorship from the board.
- The internal audit function should be separate from the risk management function to maintain perspective, independence, impartiality and provide constructive challenge.
- There must be a focal point for risk management that is a centre of excellence for implementing policies, processes and strategies and is a conduit for risk reporting.
- Managers within the business must be clear about their risk management responsibilities.
- It is the responsibility of everyone in an organisation to manage risk.
- Risk management should be applied to all organisational activities as it has a significant bearing on the fulfilment of an organisation's objectives.
- For risk management to be effective in supporting an organisation's achievement of its objectives, it must be adequately resourced.
- The external environment of an organisation influences the way it is structured and organised and in turn the way responsibility for risk management is allocated.

2.8 SUPPORT STRUCTURE

For the benefits of risk management to be realised, the process needs to be led, directed, driven and encouraged through the creation of a support structure. More specifically, a risk management team should ensure that the policies are adhered to, the process is followed, appropriate techniques are adopted, reports are issued to meet senior management and board requirements, the regulators' guidelines are adhered to and best practice is followed – all at the appropriate time. This team must also facilitate the embedding of risk management in the organisation's culture through activities such as e-learning, workshops, seminars and training. The benefits of risk management must be described and communicated across the organisation along with the steps required to achieve those benefits. To accomplish all of these management actions it is common to develop a suitable management structure.

2.8.1 Supporting factors

- A central risk function should be created and be supported by full- or part-time employees.
- These staff are commonly independent of and do not carry out audit activities.
- Staff within this function will most likely carry out the risk management techniques described in Appendix B, depending on the size and type of the organisation and whether it is within the private or public sector.
- To be effective, the central risk function should be staffed by personnel experienced in the discipline of risk management and who are familiar with the business. Appointments should only be made against detailed job descriptions.
- The induction of personnel joining the central risk function should include familiarisation with all departments within the organisation, the regulatory context and all existing processes and procedures.

2.9   EARLY WARNING INDICATORS

One of the aims of risk management is to be proactive and to anticipate potential problems. Organisations should establish early warning indicators for critical business activities to provide information on the potential sources of risk. Early warning indicators can be used as a way of tracking business sensitive issues, so that if certain predefined levels are reached, corrective action will be triggered. These early warning indicators could be applied to a range of issues such as staff turnover, liquidity, absenteeism, sickness, sales, stock levels, loss of customers, supplier default, late payments, success rate of tenders, overhead costs and revenues. For early warning indicators to be of value they must measure critical business activities and be reviewed on a regular basis. The information gathered must be accurate, and it must reach the decision-makers and be acted on.

2.9.1 Supporting factors

- Early warning indicators are established for critical business systems.
- Decision-makers, with the authority to take corrective action, examine the indicators on a regular basis.
- The information is presented in a concise, consistent manner so that it can be readily understood.

- The indicators are revised as the business, or its context, changes.
- The indicators are not purely inward looking but also measure changes in the organisation's environment.
- Greater granularity is added to the indicators where additional information will aid decision-making.
- Reports containing trend information on the indicators are kept confidential, as they are likely to contain sensitive information about the organisation.

2.10 REVIEW CYCLE

An organisation's system of internal control has a key role to play in the management of risks that have significant bearing on the fulfilment of the organisation's overall objectives. A sound system of internal control has the potential to safeguard the shareholders' investment together with the company's assets (in the private sector) or stakeholder interests (in the public sector). As with an organisation's objectives, its internal organisation and the environment within which it operates are continually evolving, so do the risks it faces. A sound and effective risk process is contingent on regular reviews of the risks that the organisation is facing and the policies, processes and strategies it is adopting to manage them.

2.10.1 Supporting factors

- Organisations should review the effectiveness of their risk management policies and processes on a regular cycle. Management should provide assurance to the board that a review has been undertaken and report on the findings.
- A process should be defined for scoping and conducting these reviews and on the structure, content and format of the reports.
- Reports should highlight any significant risks and the effectiveness of the response actions in managing those risks.
- Any significant control failings or weaknesses identified should be discussed in the reports, including the impact that they have had or may have on the organisation and the response actions that have been put in place.
- Reviews should be conducted according to the timing of internal audits, annual reports, and external inspections by a regulator or shareholder meetings.

2.11 OVERCOMING BARRIERS TO M_o_R

There needs to be recognition that even though an organisation has risk management policies, processes and strategies in place, this will not automatically lead to robust, effective and efficient risk management practices. It is commonly accepted that there are a series of barriers or obstacles to the implementation of risk management that need to be addressed to secure the benefits of risk management. A lack of comprehension of these barriers can restrict an organisation in improving the maturity of its processes.

2.11.1 Supporting factors

- Senior management commitment to risk management should be established otherwise middle and lower management will be without adequate support.
- Training, knowledge of risk management practices, and formal risk tools and techniques should be in place otherwise risk management implementation may be inhibited.
- An adequate budget for risk management should be in place. Inadequate resources will curtail activities and may suggest that risk management is not considered important.
- The most effective risk management practices are those that reward productive risk management behaviour and investment.

2.12 SUPPORTIVE CULTURE

Organisations should establish the right culture to support management of risk throughout the organisation. Culture is understood here to mean 'the way things are done'. A supportive culture will be one that embeds risk management into day-to-day operations. The culture will recognise how beneficial risk management is considered to be by the board. The degree of support for risk management will reside somewhere on the continuum between doing the minimum to satisfy governance requirements through to driving business improvement to become a market leader. The culture will include: assigning roles and responsibilities; agreement on which activities will include risk assessments (e.g. constructing new premises, entering into joint ventures or outsourcing IT); the processes that will be adopted; the reporting frequency; escalation; the use of tools and techniques; and the templates to be employed. The culture will be embodied in the organisation's overall risk management policies.

2.12.1 Supporting factors

- A leading member of the board should sponsor risk management.
- Senior management should demonstrate through its policies and actions the necessary commitment to risk management and the fostering of a climate of trust so that risks can be openly shared and discussed without fear of retribution.
- A management culture that is quick to penalise staff, focuses on the negatives, always wants to apportion blame, and does not want to spend time looking at root causes, hampers the embedding of risk management.
- Organisations should use incentives as well as disincentive systems. The most effective cultures balance control with reward. Staff should be rewarded for identifying ways of reducing threats and optimising opportunities.
- A code of conduct, human resource policies and performance reward systems should be established to support effective risk management.
- Organisations should embed risk management throughout their operating divisions so that it becomes part of day-to-day activities. This can be achieved by way of communication mechanisms such as e-learning, seminars, case studies, lessons learned and company exchanges.

2.13 CONTINUAL IMPROVEMENT

Although risk management reviews will enable organisations to understand the effectiveness of risk response planning on current or recently completed activities, it will not equip management with an adequate understanding of their risk maturity to enable them to plan and implement a step change in their risk management practices. Organisations that are interested in continual improvement should develop strategies to improve their risk maturity.

This can be accomplished by the use of a maturity model to understand the adequacies of current practices and the improvements that are possible. Independent parties can carry out benchmarking against a maturity model. This will provide an informed, impartial, unbiased and independent perspective devoid of personal agendas and unaffected by previous decision-making.

2.13.1 Supporting factors

- Organisations should review their practices against a maturity model to determine the level of maturity they have attained and the corresponding benefits that can be expected.

- A realistic plan should be prepared to enable progression of risk management practices to the next level in the maturity model.

- Prior to implementing a plan, the benefits to be obtained from reaching the next level of maturity should be weighed against the resources that would be required.

- Moving from one maturity model level to the next should be managed as a project with clear objectives, resources and timeframe, and instigated against a business case.

Management of risk approach

3

3 Management of risk approach

3.1 INTRODUCTION

The way in which the principles described in the previous chapter are implemented will vary from organisation to organisation. Collectively they provide a base on which risk management practices for an organisation can be developed. These practices describe how risk management will be undertaken throughout the organisation – the M_o_R approach.

To capture and communicate these practices it is common to create a management of risk approach composed of a series of living documents called:

- Risk Management Policy
- Risk Management Process Guide
- Risk Management Strategies
- Risk Registers
- Issue Logs.

In simple terms these documents describe how things should be done and should, over time, be integrated into an organisation's culture. They describe the activities to be undertaken, the sequence in which these are undertaken and the roles and responsibilities necessary for their delivery.

The purpose of this chapter is to describe the purpose and content of these documents. Document outlines for each document are provided in Appendix A.

3.2 RISK MANAGEMENT POLICY

3.2.1 Purpose

To communicate how risk management will be implemented throughout an organisation (or part of an organisation) to support the realisation of its strategic objectives.

3.2.2 Background

Small organisations may have a single policy describing the risk management practices that will be implemented throughout the organisation. For larger organisations there may be a hierarchy of policies. The policy designed for the group headquarters would be supported by policies prepared for (and tailored to suit):

- Individual companies within the group
- Divisions within each company

- Portfolios of programmes and programmes of interlinked projects undertaken by each division
- Individual projects and operations undertaken by each division.

The policy is the method of communicating why risk management should be undertaken and how it relates to the corporate objectives, and it provides a common language. It strives to accomplish uniformity across risk management processes; it aims to remove ambiguity about the organisation's risk appetite and when to escalate risks, and describes the format, timing and content of reports. Depending on the organisation's financial management practices the policy may also describe the financial benefits of risk management together with a budget for risk management. The policy can contain a detailed description of the risk management process or it can provide a high-level view with a fuller description being provided in a separate document. For larger companies a policy may have several supplementary documents that have a parent/child relationship.

3.2.3 Composition

Typically a policy will include:

- Introduction
- Risk appetite and capacity
- Risk tolerance thresholds
- Procedure for escalation
- Roles and responsibilities
- Glossary of terms
- Risk management process
- Early warning indicators
- Tools and techniques to support the process
- When risk management should be implemented
- Reporting
- Budget
- Quality assurance
- Annual review
- Additional information sources.

It is common for the policy to have a number of annexes containing additional detailed information to support the policy. The annexes will vary according to the nature of the organisation.

Introduction

The introduction will describe the purpose of the policy. It will name the owner of the policy, provide an explanation of the relationship with other policies, and describe the benefits of implementing risk management, the principles and objectives of risk management, and compliance requirements. It will advise that the policy should be read in conjunction with the Risk Management Process Guide and individual Risk Management Strategies.

Risk appetite and capacity

Risk appetite driven by capacity

This section will describe the organisation's risk appetite (based on its capacity). Risk appetite plays a vital role in supporting an organisation's objectives and orchestrating risk management activities. Risk appetite refers to an organisation's unique attitude towards risk taking, which in turn dictates the amount of risk that it considers acceptable. As a result, risk appetite refers to an organisation's willingness to tolerate a particular level of exposure to specific risks or risk groups. This appetite is also logically a function of the organisation's capacity to bear risk, which should not be exceeded. Risk appetite is an essential element of risk governance and internal controls. It provides a framework for the business to operate within, in terms of what is and is not acceptable to the organisation. In certain regulated industries constraints are imposed on risk appetite as a result of the capital levels that need to be maintained to comply with regulatory capital requirements. The board and senior management are responsible for defining their organisation's risk appetite as an integral part of business planning, having once determined its risk bearing capacity.

Risk appetite has a series of benefits in that it helps staff understand the relative significance of the risks faced by the organisation. Organisations that effectively articulate their risk appetite:

- Provide themselves with a policy for considering and approving levels of risk taking
- Prioritise risk management action by focusing response planning, monitoring and control activities on the risks that can cause the most harm
- Place greater emphasis on risk controls to reduce contingency sums and so achieve a more efficient allocation of capital across the organisation
- Better insulate themselves against any shock to future earnings
- Place themselves in a better position to allocate scarce resources and take advantage of beneficial changes in the insurance market

- Leave themselves room for creativity within acceptable limits
- Reduce the possibility of exposure to exceeding capacity due to a lack of awareness
- Make better decisions by changing business direction when it is estimated that attempting to mitigate assessed risks would not bring the risks within acceptable limits.

Risk tolerance thresholds

It is common for a number of practical steps to be undertaken to apply a risk appetite to an organisation's risk management practices. The key step is the creation of risk tolerance thresholds within business units and their functional units. These thresholds represent levels of exposure, which with appropriate approvals, can be exceeded, but which when exceeded, will trigger some form of response (e.g. reporting the situation to senior management for action).

These steps include (but are not limited to):

- Gaining senior management buy-in to the concept of appetite in order to establish acceptance of tolerance thresholds
- Review by business unit and functional area management, to consider, interpret and decide on threshold limits for their units and function(s)
- Development by the central risk function to implement system limits, monitoring and exception reports, thresholds and early warning indicators, as appropriate.

It is anticipated that there will be a series of direct and indirect costs arising from establishing thresholds and these might relate to:

- Board and senior management time – agreeing the thresholds to support the defined appetite.
- IT staff time – supporting risk management activities.
- Risk management time spent by the central risk management team – creating proposals for tolerance thresholds, facilitation of thresholds, documentation, review and monitoring.
- Internal audit/external consultants – review, technical support, assistance and assurance over appetite setting and resetting.

Procedure for escalation

This section will describe the escalation procedure to be adopted for the activity or area of the business to which the policy relates. For each perspective (or major activity), a risk escalation procedure should be developed whereby management teams (at these perspectives) are advised of the tolerance thresholds (see above) to which they are required to adhere. In the event that a single risk, group of risks or activity exceeds the agreed threshold, then the results should be escalated to a senior manager in accordance with pre-agreed procedures. The senior manager will be responsible for either deciding a course of action or escalating the information to a more senior level. The thresholds are commonly financial but may relate to other success criteria such as timeframe, operational requirements or regulatory compliance matters.

Roles and responsibilities

This section will describe the risk management duties of specific roles within the organisation. This will typically involve the risk champion, board of directors (or similar in the public sector), internal audit function, central risk function, risk manager, programme, project and operational managers, and members of staff.

- **The board:** collectively or a member of the board must approve the funding for risk management and must ensure that decision-making is supported by risk management. For risk management to be effective, it must be championed at board level. As a board's remit is typically to grow a business and keep it aligned and responsive to the marketplace, the approach commonly adopted combines acquisitions, divestments, outsourcing, organisational change and investments. Risk management must support all of these decisions.

- **The internal audit committee:** will be responsible for supporting the definition of the organisation-wide risk appetite and for overseeing the preparation of risk policies, the risk process guide and risk tolerance levels for divisions or departments. The committee will also carry out audits of the application and effectiveness of risk management overall and will report to the board on their findings. It is not the responsibility of the internal audit function to carry out risk management. It must remain independent to retain its impartiality and ability to report objectively. The internal audit committee typically contributes to the content of the annual review.

- **The risk committee:** will be responsible for advising the board on risk management and fostering a risk management culture within the organisation that emphasises and demonstrates the benefits of a risk-based approach to internal control and management of the organisation. The committee will make appropriate recommendations to the board on all significant matters relating to the organisation's risk strategy and policies. It will keep under review the effectiveness of the organisation's risk management approach. This will include: consideration of risk audit reports on the key business areas to assess the level of business risk exposure; consideration of any major findings of any regulators and internal/external audit's risk management reviews and management's response; and an assessment of the risks of new ventures and other strategic initiatives. It will review the organisation's operational risk exposures in relation to the board's risk appetite and the organisation's capital adequacy. The committee will consider the maturity of risk management practices and make appropriate recommendations to the board. It will also be responsible for considering whether the public disclosure of information regarding the organisation's risk management policies and key risk exposures is in accordance with the statutory requirement and financial reporting standards. Depending on the size of an organisation, the risk committee may be supported (or replaced) by a central risk function.

- **The central risk function:** may be performed by an individual (as a full- or part-time role) or by a team. The remit is wide ranging and requires experienced personnel to implement it. The bullet point list below is a guide and may be expanded or reduced to suit the prevalent circumstances:

  - Advise senior management of the benefits of risk management, and where appropriate develop a business case and agree a budget for risk management personnel
  - Prepare or support the preparation of risk management policies, the process, and advise on techniques to be used and the tools to be acquired or developed
  - Develop a maturity model to establish the organisation's current risk management capabilities and where it aspires to reach
  - Embed risk management by providing seminars, arranging e-learning and risk management training and facilitating workshops
  - Advise on when risk management activity should be undertaken, carry out or supervise the implementation of the risk process on programmes and projects, and prepare Risk Management Strategies
  - Provide reports on programmes or individual organisational activities to senior management
  - Advise on risk appetite, escalation, contingencies and risk capacity

- Support the completion of statements of internal control (SIC) and annual review reports, and answer internal and external auditors' questions
- Implement or commission risk healthchecks
- Collect and disseminate papers describing expected changes in the context of the organisation
- Advise on compliance with the Combined Code and regulatory requirements
- Promulgate a consistent approach by preparing templates
- Liaise with the legal, procurement, finance and programme departments and develop an enterprise-wide capability.

■ **A risk manager** (sometimes referred to as a risk facilitator or risk coordinator): commonly drives the implementation of the risk management process on a particular organisational activity, typically undertaking: stakeholder analysis; the facilitation of risk workshops/meetings; the preparation of scales of impact and probability; the construction of Risk Registers; the analysis of alternative options; quantitative analysis; and report preparation. This is by no means an exhaustive list.

■ **Programme, project and operational managers:** will be responsible for implementing the risk policy prepared by the internal audit committee (appropriate to their level), preparing individual risk strategies and response plans for specific activities, assigning personnel to risk management roles (such as risk manager), embedding risk management, escalating risks above an agreed tolerance level to senior management, risk reporting, agreeing and managing risk contingencies, chairing progress meetings including monitoring risk response actions, and coordinating their activities with other organisational activities.

Glossary of terms

For risk management to be effective all participants must speak the same language. It is important that a common vocabulary is adopted where the agreed meanings are unambiguous and reflect best practice. This may sound trivial, but the application of risk management will quickly unravel if the terms in use mean different things to different participants. A glossary is included at the end of this guide for adoption as a common language.

Risk management process

The policy will cross-refer to the process that will be adopted in terms of the steps in the process and when it will be applied. The process is commonly recorded in a

separate document called a Risk Management Process Guide. A generic process is described in Chapter 4.

Early warning indicators

A series of early warning indicators can be generated that can be used to measure a change in business critical areas. There are a considerable number that can be used and a small sample is included below. To be effective they need to be monitored on a very regular basis and the findings presented in such a way that the information can be quickly assimilated.

- Liquidity
- Turnover
- Profitability
- Staff turnover
- Project failure/success
- Contract penalties imposed
- Lost bids
- Insurance premium increases
- Legal actions
- Media coverage
- Regulator penalties.

Tools and techniques to support the process

This section cross-refers to the Risk Management Process Guide. The subject is not discussed in detail here to prevent the Risk Management Policy and the Process Guide providing conflicting information and to avoid the assumption being made that the subject is addressed elsewhere.

When risk management should be implemented

The policy may describe the activities that require risk management. The degree of risk management activity involved will vary according to the organisational perspective from which the activities are being undertaken. Chapter 6 explains when and how risk management should be applied throughout an organisation, from the strategic, programme, project and operational perspectives.

Reporting

This section will describe the purpose, frequency, structure and content of reports.

Budget

This section will describe how risk management will be supported across the organisation. There are no hard and fast rules to determine a budget for risk management as circumstances vary from organisation to organisation. A budget for risk management personnel or support from an external provider is generally correlated to the board's or senior management's perception of the value of risk management and its contribution to bottom-line performance. The trigger for a risk budget to be increased tends to be when:

- An organisation has suffered a major financial loss that could have been avoided in full or in part
- The organisation has had its reputation tarnished
- The regulatory regime has tightened
- The regulator has imposed a fine
- Hedging has been unsuccessful
- A contract failed and penalties were imposed
- A major shareholder raises concerns
- A major programme or project has overrun, or
- The market within which the organisation operates has become far more competitive and margins have been eroded.

Quality assurance

Quality assurance will relate to document control, version control, saving documents, common structure and format, amendment post-regulatory change, consistency between documents, sign-off, review, ownership and feedback.

Annual review

At least annually organisations should review their risk management practices to understand what has not been working as well as expected. Following the review, actions should be undertaken to put in place planned improvements to enhance practices. The internal audit committee commonly undertakes the review by interviewing the central risk function and senior management and reviewing risk management documentation.

3.2.4 Activities

In simple terms the policy must be written, reviewed and subsequently signed off by a member of the board or the audit committee. Policies should be sent with a separate cover page requiring confirmation that the recipient has received, read and understood the content. To be of value, policies need to be updated on a regular basis and their application needs to be monitored. Special attention needs to be paid to communicating the benefits of risk management with examples, to reinforce the significance and relevance of risk management to the organisation. There needs to be an explicit and transparent relationship between risk management principles and the policy.

3.2.5 Relationship

If the policy is one of a hierarchical set of policies, care must be taken to ensure that the policies do not contain conflicting information and that the roles and responsibilities unique to the policy are correct. With this in mind, they should be updated at the same time, on a regular cycle, and they should clearly explain the hierarchical relationship between the policies. The reporting requirements within one policy must reflect and correlate with the reporting requirements in the other policies.

3.3 RISK MANAGEMENT PROCESS GUIDE

3.3.1 Purpose

To describe the series of steps (from Identify through to Implement) and their respective associated activities, necessary to implement risk management.

3.3.2 Background

The process should be tailored to the organisation and be suitable for all types of activity across the organisation. It should be applicable to all levels of management and activity. This document should describe a best practice approach that will support a consistent method and deliver effective risk management. The audit committee, risk committee or risk function is normally responsible for determining the process that the organisation adopts. The process guide is commonly one of the documents used to review compliance against internal controls. It should be reviewed and updated at least annually and always after the release of new national standards and new legislation affecting corporate governance, internal controls, financial management or the regulatory regime.

3.3.3 Composition

Typically a process document will include as a minimum:

- Introduction
- Roles and responsibilities
- Steps in the process
- Tools and techniques
- Templates
- Glossary of terms.

It may also include:

- Early warning indicators
- How contingencies will be defined
- Owners of contingencies.

risk identification
— diff at diff levels eg. horizon-scanning
at strategic level

24 | Management of risk approach

Introduction

The introduction will state the purpose and the owner of the document, the activities that it is intended to support, its relationship with the Risk Management Policy and the requirement for it to be read in conjunction with individual Risk Management Strategies.

Roles and responsibilities

The Risk Management Process Guide must set out:

- Who has overall responsibility for the process
- The management structure for risk management
- Who is responsible for updating the process
- Who is responsible for risk management tools
- The frequency that risk reviews are carried out.

Steps in the process

A generic process is described in Chapter 4 that can form the basis for this section of the guide. This section should describe the steps, their purpose, the activities to be carried out within each step, and the respective inputs and outputs.

A key component of the risk process is risk identification. Due to the differing nature of the risks facing an organisation at different levels of the organisational structure, a different risk identification approach is required at each level. Whereas operational risks (for instance) are commonly concerned with very short-term problems around manufacturing resilience, strategic risks relate to a longer timeframe. 'Horizon scanning' is an approach that is gaining in popularity as a means of identifying future threats and opportunities. It may be defined as the systematic examination of potential threats, opportunities and likely future developments which are at the margins of current thinking and planning. As it focuses on the future, horizon scanning is concerned with events that may have a positive or negative effect on strategic and long-range planning. This approach provides a method for 'stress testing' business planning and strategic thinking. Organisations undertake horizon scanning to improve resilience and capability by anticipating and preparing for new threats and opportunities. In many instances the approach challenges and stretches current thinking on future trends and technologies.

Tools and techniques

The process may describe the tools and techniques to be used to support each of the individual steps; these will be covered in greater detail in the individual Risk Management Strategies for programmes, projects and operations. Techniques are described in Appendix B of this guide.

Templates

This section will describe the full set of templates available along with their purpose and location. Instructions on their specific use are reserved for the individual Risk Management Strategies. Templates are an important way to ensure consistent reporting and ease the amalgamation of multiple reports to produce a single overall report (for example when 'rolling-up' multiple project risk reports into a single programme report).

Glossary of terms

Either there should be a cross-reference to the glossary contained within the Risk Management Policy or the same terms should be repeated here.

3.3.4 Activities

The process should be sufficiently generic in nature so that it can be applied to the majority of risk management activities in the organisation.

3.3.5 Relationship

The process must be consistent with the Risk Management Policy, the risk management objectives and the individual Risk Management Strategies.

3.4 RISK MANAGEMENT STRATEGY

3.4.1 Purpose

The purpose of a Risk Management Strategy is to describe for a particular organisational activity the specific risk management activities that will be undertaken.

3.4.2 Background

Strategies are typically prepared for, say, a programme, a project, office relocation, organisational change, outsourcing, a revision to key processes, or the introduction of new software. It must be emphasised that the strategy is tailored to each specific activity, while at the same time reflecting the process document and the hierarchy of policy documents. The strategy should be prepared before embarking on any risk management activity. Where appropriate the strategy should relate to the OGC Gateway Review Strategy Process for public sector programmes and projects and alternative assurance and approval processes (such as the RIBA Plan of Work) for the private sector.

3.4.3 Composition

Typically a strategy document will include:

- Introduction

- Outline of the activity
- Roles and responsibilities
- The process
- Scales for estimating probability and impact
- Probability
- Impact
- Expected value
- Proximity
- Risk response category
- Budget required
- Tools and techniques
- Templates
- Early warning indicators
- Timing of risk management activities
- Reporting
- Glossary of terms
- Checklists and prompt lists.

Specie for each activity

Introduction

The introduction will state the purpose and owner of the document, the activity to which it relates, where questions should be referred, why the document must be followed, and any other documents that should be read in conjunction with the strategy.

Outline of the activity

The outline of the activity is a summary description of the organisational activity to which risk management will be applied. The outline typically describes the objectives, budget, timeframe, scope, sponsor, stakeholders, approval process and primary tasks. It may also refer to the location of more detailed documents.

Roles and responsibilities

It is common for an organisational chart to be included in the strategy, describing the roles (and the individuals carrying out those roles) for the organisational activity to which the risk strategy relates.

The chart can illustrate reporting lines, contractual relationships, levels of authority, routes for escalation and owners of contingency, together with owners of the Risk Management Policy, Process Guide and the Risk Management Strategy. It will also describe the duties of the risk manager and the primary participants in the process.

The process

This section of the strategy will describe the risk management process that will be adopted and will refer to the Risk Management Process Guide. It will state what departures (if any) have been made from the steps described in the process guide and why they were necessary, or it will state that the guide will be followed.

Scales for estimating probability and impact

Probability impact grids should be developed specifically for each activity to ensure that the scales of cost and time (for instance) are relevant to the cost and timeframe associated with that specific activity. These grids should not be deemed final: it may be necessary to adjust the ranges to suit the circumstances as the risks and their impacts are identified and evolve. These subjects are discussed in more detail below.

Probability

Probability is the evaluated likelihood of a particular threat or opportunity actually happening, including a consideration of the frequency with which this may arise.

The pre-response/inherent probability initially assigned to a risk is based on no response action being in place. Once response actions are implemented it may be appropriate to record the post-response/residual probability.

It is helpful for the purpose of prioritising management effort to adopt scales for classifying probability. The most common scale is composed of five bands, labelled 'very high', 'high', 'medium', 'low' and 'very low'. Providing a set of criteria against each of these labels facilitates a common understanding of the categories. For example:

Table 3.1 Example of risk probability framework

Probability	Criteria	Likelihood
Very high	> 75%	Almost certainly will occur
High	51–75%	More likely to occur than not
Medium	26–50%	Fairly likely to occur
Low	6–25%	Unlikely to occur
Very low	0–5%	Extremely unlikely or virtually impossible

It may also be useful to provide numerical equivalents, for example:

Table 3.2 Numerical equivalents

Probability	Numerical Equivalent
Very high	Less than one chance in a hundred ($<10^{-2}$)
High	Less than one chance in a thousand ($<10^{-3}$)
Medium	Less than one chance in ten thousand ($<10^{-4}$)
Low	Less than one chance in a hundred thousand ($<10^{-5}$)
Very low	One in a million (10^{-6})

Another view is to consider the likelihood of a risk occurring within a time period, for example:

Table 3.3 Time periods

Probability	Likelihood	Time period
Very high	Almost certain	Likely to occur once within three months
High	Probable	Likely to occur once within a one-year period
Medium	Possible	Likely to occur once within a 10-year period
Low	Remote	Unlikely to occur within a 10-year period
Very low	Very remote	Unlikely to occur in a 50-year period

Impact

Impact is the result of a particular threat or opportunity actually occurring.

The pre-mitigation impact initially assigned to a risk is based on no mitigation action being in place. Once mitigation actions are implemented it may be appropriate to record the post-mitigation/residual impact.

Impacts on an organisational activity are usually considered in terms of the organisational objectives and hence examine the impact on:

- Costs
- Timescale
- Quality/requirements.

If the organisational objectives are broader, then an assessment of impact may look at the other objectives such as reputation, compliance, maintainability, accessibility and reliability.

The range selected for each band should suit the programme, project or operation being conducted and reflect the business sensitivity in terms of the objectives. The cost impact ranges adopted for a small project may be shown as per Table 3.4. This range would clearly be inappropriate for a project budgeted at £5 million, however.

Table 3.4 Cost impact ranges

Impact	Cost
Very high	> £750K
High	£500K – 750K
Medium	£250K – £500K
Low	£50K – 250K
Very low	< £50K

Table 3.5 describes a possible impact banding for a short duration project. This range would most likely be inappropriate for a project of more than five years, however. As with cost impact bands, time bands must reflect the particular circumstances of the project under examination.

Table 3.5 Time band impact

Impact	Time
Very high	> 25 days
High	20 days – 25 days
Medium	10 days – 20 days
Low	5 days – 10 days
Very low	< 5 days

Table 3.6 describes a possible impact banding for risks that may reduce the delivery of the requirements for an activity. These descriptions would typically be made more specific to suit the nature of the deliverables of the activity.

Table 3.6 Impact on requirements

Impact	Requirements
Very high	Major shortfall in any of the critical requirements
High	Shortfall in any of the critical requirements
Medium	Shortfall in multiple requirements
Low	Shortfall in ancillary requirements
Very low	Minor shortfall in ancillary requirements

Some types of risk, such as financial risk, can be estimated in numerical terms; others, such as adverse publicity, can only be estimated in subjective ways. Whichever approach is adopted, an attempt should be made to convert these estimates into a monetary value as a means of providing direct comparison.

Expected value

The expected value is calculated by multiplying the average impact by the probability percentage (where this is used). Once again this is a pre-mitigation estimate that takes no account of any future risk management action to reduce the impact or the probability.

By totalling the expected values for all of the risks associated with an organisational activity, an understanding of the total risk exposure faced by that particular activity can be calculated. Caution should be exercised when reporting this figure to management as effectively the figure represents the mean value and there is approximately a 50% chance that this figure will be exceeded.

Proximity

Risks are time based and are not constant. They will occur at particular times and the severity of their impact will vary according to when they occur. This time factor is known as the 'proximity' of the risk. Whereas an understanding of a risk's probability and impact informs management of the importance of a risk, understanding a risk's proximity informs management of its urgency. Knowing proximity will also help to identify the appropriate response and the required trigger and timing of the response.

Risk response category

There are a number of ways to respond to a risk, and these will depend on whether the risk is a perceived threat or an opportunity.

Directive / Preventive / Detective / Corrective [handwritten]

Table 3.7 describes the alternative responses for a threat.

Table 3.7 Threat responses

Reduction [*Control*]	Proactive actions taken to reduce: ■ The probability of the event occurring, by performing some form of control (see below for the four types of control available), or ■ The impact of the event should it occur.
Removal	Typically involves changing one aspect of the organisational activity, i.e. changing the scope, procurement route, supplier or sequence of activities.
Transfer	A third party takes on responsibility for an aspect of the threat (see below for the four traditional categories of transfer). *Fixed price/firm price* [handwritten]
Retention	A conscious and deliberate decision is taken to retain the threat, having discerned that it is more economical to do so than to attempt a risk response action, for example. The threat should continue to be monitored to ensure that it remains tolerable. *— do nothing* [handwritten]
Share	Modern procurement methods commonly entail a form of risk sharing through the application of a pain/gain formula: both parties share the gain (within pre-agreed limits) if the cost is less than the cost plan; or share the pain (again within pre-agreed limits) if the cost plan is exceeded. Several industries include risk sharing principles within their contracts with third parties.

pre-agreed limits : share pain/gain [handwritten]

Table 3.8 lists the types of control available.

Table 3.8 Control options

Control	Description
Directive	Designed to ensure that the particular outcome is achieved. Typically associated with health and safety. For example: wearing protective clothing during the performance of dangerous tasks, or insisting on staff being trained before starting a project.
Preventive	Designed to limit the possibility of an undesirable outcome being realised. The majority of controls fall into this category. The separation of duty to prevent fraud is an example.
Detective	Designed to identify occasions where undesirable outcomes have been realised. Their impact is after the event, so they are only appropriate where it is possible to accept the loss or damage incurred. Examples include stock or asset checks, reconciliations and post-implementation reviews that identify lessons learned from projects for future application.
Corrective	Designed to correct undesirable outcomes that have been realised. They provide a route of recourse to achieve some recovery against loss or damage. An example of this would be the design of contract terms to allow recovery of overpayment. Insurance can be regarded as a form of corrective control.

Table 3.9 provides examples of the types of transfer that occur in practice.

Table 3.9 Transfer categories

Categories of transfer	Description
Insurance	When a premium is paid to an insurance company, the contract indemnifies the insured against the associated financial costs of any loss. Not all risks can be insured; the following characteristics should be present: ■ The loss must be measurable in monetary terms ■ The risk must be one of a number of similar risks ■ There must be no prospect of gain or profit ■ The loss must be fortuitous, i.e. entirely accidental ■ The risk cannot be illegal or immoral ■ There must be an insurable interest, i.e. the insured must be the person who will incur the loss.
Self-insurance	When the cost of the loss is borne by the organisation, for example by setting aside reserves or funds to meet the cost of the loss.
Insurance captive	A captive insurance company is one formed to participate in the insurance portfolio of its parent organisation. This approach is normally restricted to larger organisations.
Contractual transfer	When the financial consequence of the threat is transferred to a third party by means of appropriate clauses in a contract. The most usual clauses are known as indemnity clauses, exclusion clauses or hold harmless clauses. To be effective, such clauses have to form part of a legally binding contract where the terms of the clause were brought to the attention of the third party during negotiations.

For an opportunity, the responses are set out in Table 3.10.

Table 3.10 Opportunity responses

Realisation	*Identifying and seizing an opportunity* The realisation of an opportunity ensures that potential improvements to an organisational activity are delivered. For example, if there is an opportunity to complete a project early and reduce the headcount, the realisation of the opportunity would be to achieve the reduced costs possible through a lower-than-planned headcount.
Enhancement	*Seizing and improving on an identified opportunity* Enhancement of an opportunity refers to both the realisation of an opportunity and achieving additional gains over and above the opportunity. An example may be negotiating a lower rental figure for existing occupied premises and restructuring the organisation to reduce the floor space required. Or it may include achieving financial gain from finishing a project early and gaining additional revenue from deploying the released resources on another project.
Exploitation	*Identifying and seizing multiple benefits* Exploitation refers to changing an activity's scope, supplier or specification to achieve a beneficial outcome without changing the objectives or specification. An example is where a contractor on a fixed-price contract manages to obtain a lower price from an alternative supplier on *multiple* subcontracts, while maintaining the desired specification.

[handwritten margin notes: "follow over it; make it happen", "extra activity to make it better", "more than one are benefit"]

Budget required

The strategy may describe either a risk budget or an allocation of man-days for risk management support for the organisational activity. This support may be from the central risk management team or an individual practitioner.

Tools and techniques

The strategy should describe the preferred technique(s) to be used for each step in the process. It should also describe the tool(s) to be used and the software that will be adopted. This is particularly important where a risk database will be used and a number of individuals will be inputting data. It may go as far as to describe which fields are to be populated and how.

Templates

Templates might include a Risk Register, Risk Progress Report, probability impact grids, dashboard report pages, risk response sheets or budget spreadsheets. Their aim is to produce consistency and ensure that certain information is captured. Templates are particularly important when a series of projects are being implemented as part of a programme and the reports from individual projects have to be rolled up into a single report. Unless the information has been collected and recorded in a consistent manner, rolling up the information into a single report will be needlessly time-consuming and may require more management time than is necessary.

Early warning indicators

The early warning indicators will be selected for their relevancy to the organisational activity that the strategy supports and will be included in the reports.

Timing of risk management activities

Risk Management Strategies will record the lifecycle of the activity including the individual stages, review points and overall duration. Risk Management Strategies for projects or programmes will typically describe the risk management activities that will be carried out at each gateway review (or lifecycle review point).

Reporting

This section will reflect the requirements of the relevant policy, describe the reports that are to be produced, and record the purpose, timing and recipients of the reports. There is a growing use of dashboards within reports for the ongoing monitoring of risk exposure. This enables the current status to be combined with trend analysis (for example, how does the current position differ from the last three months?). A dashboard is a graphical representation of the 'headlines' of a risk report to enable senior management or the board to very quickly assimilate the most significant issues of the report. The dashboard will highlight those areas that give rise for concern (downside risks) or show promise (upside risks). A dashboard may be any combination of a pie chart, histograms, radar charts, distribution curves, risk maps, Red/Amber/Green/Blue (RAGB) reports or tables. A dashboard may be produced for a whole organisation, portfolio, programme, project or operational area. As with all reports, their value depends on the quality of the information that they contain.

Glossary of terms

Either there should be a cross-reference to the glossary contained within the Risk Management Policy or the same terms should be repeated here.

Checklists and prompt lists

Checklists should be specific to the activity. For instance, a rail risk checklist is of little value on a nuclear programme and vice versa. Prompt lists tend to be generic, as they look at risk categories, and therefore do not need to be activity specific.

3.4.4 Activities

It is important that all activity participants understand why risk management information is required; the knowledge will guide them in the information gathering process. Determine what the sponsor is particularly interested in. Is it confidence in achieving the schedule? Is it to choose between three competing options? Is it to understand the anticipated benefits of delivering an investment early? Is it to discern an appropriate contingency for a capital project? Or, is it to understand the risks of developing a new product? All of these end goals have a totally different focus and if the wrong approach is taken at the outset, appropriate modelling cannot be undertaken. The organisation's ability to implement the strategy will be largely dictated by the education and experience of its staff members and their competence in undertaking the steps in the process, applying techniques, using tools, analysing the results and making well-reasoned judgements. Inaccurate and misleading information can be more harmful than no information at all. Sufficient resources must be available to carry out the activities described in the plan. Risk management is a professional role and for some activities it will be necessary to appoint a specialist to support the initiative.

3.4.5 Relationship

The Risk Management Strategy must be coordinated with the Risk Management Policy (or Policies) and the Risk Management Process Guide.

3.5 RISK REGISTER

3.5.1 Purpose

To capture and maintain information on all of the identified threats and opportunities relating to a specific organisational activity.

3.5.2 Background

Each organisation will need to decide on the precise content of its own Risk Register. The layout of the register (typically reading from left to right) should reflect the sequence in which information is captured. If the recognised purpose of the Risk Register is to collect sufficient information to enable risk response planning and subsequent control, then this will dictate the information contained in the register. For document management purposes the register should carry a title (reflecting the organisational activity) date, date last updated, version number, author and file reference.

3.5.3 Composition

Typically a Risk Register will include:

- Risk identifier
- Risk category
- Risk cause
- Risk event (threat or opportunity)
- Risk effect (description in words of the impact)
- Probability (pre-response action)
- Probability (post-response action)
- Impact (pre-response action)
- Impact (post-response action)
- Expected value (pre-response action)
- Expected value (post-response action)
- Proximity
- Risk response categories
- Risk response actions
- Residual risk
- Risk status
- Risk owner
- Risk actionee.

Risk identifier

It is important that every risk entered into the Risk Register can be uniquely identified. This will typically be provided by a numeric or alpha-numeric value.

Risk category

When compiling a Risk Register it may be helpful to structure it using risk categories. The categories may be derived from a risk breakdown structure or a risk prompt list. If no risks have been recorded against a particular category then this will provide an immediate indication that the identification process might not have been as thorough as it should have been. Where categories do not have risks identified against them, they should be re-examined. The categories should be specific to the organisational activity under examination.

A sample set of categories follow that are indicative of a strategic level risk assessment. However, they would require significant modification for a project, for example.

- Strategic/commercial
- Economic/financial/market
- Legal/contractual/regulatory
- Organisational management/human factors
- Equality/discrimination
- Political/societal factors
- Environmental factors/acts of God (force majeure)
- Technical/operational/infrastructure.

Risk cause, event, and effect

An important aspect of identifying risk is being able to provide a clear and unambiguous expression of each risk. A useful way of expressing risk is to consider the following aspect of each risk:

- **Risk cause.** This should describe the source of the risk, i.e. the event or situation that gives rise to the risk. These are often referred to as risk drivers. They are not risks in themselves, but the potential trigger points for risk. These may be either internal or external to the organisational activity under consideration.
- **Risk event.** This should describe the area of uncertainty in terms of the threat or the opportunity.
- **Risk effect.** This should describe the impact that the risk would have on the organisational activity should the risk materialise.

Using a car journey as a simple example: a nail in a tyre is the cause, a flat tyre from the puncture is the risk event (threat), and the effect is arriving late at the destination. Typically when the Risk Register is a spreadsheet, the cause, risk event and effect are captured in separate columns to aid segregation and clarity.

Probability

The probability recorded will be selected from within the scales described in the Risk Management Strategy. Where appropriate record pre- and post-response action probabilities.

Impact

The impact recorded will be selected from within the scales described in the Risk Management Strategy. Where appropriate, record pre- and post-response action impacts.

Expected value

The expected value is calculated by multiplying the average impact by the probability percentage (where this is used).

Proximity

The proximity column within the register will state the date when the threat or opportunity is anticipated to materialise.

Risk response category

The risk response category will be selected from the options described in the Risk Management Strategy.

Risk response action

Having decided on the most appropriate category for responding to the risk, then the actual action to be taken also needs to be recorded together with any trigger dates.

Residual risk

It is common for risk responses not to be fully effective, in that they do not remove the risk in its entirety. This leaves a residual risk remaining. If the original risk was significant and the risk response was only partially successful, the remaining risk can be considerable.

Risk status

The most commonly adopted terms to describe the status of a risk are:

- **Active:** the risk is still live and relevant to the organisational activity.
- **Closed:** either the risk can no longer happen or have an impact on the activity, or it has materialised and has been transferred onto the Issue Log for action.

Risk owner

This will be a named individual who is responsible for the management and control of all aspects of the risks assigned to them, including the implementation of the selected actions to address the threats or to maximise the opportunities. It should be noted that owners of the probability reduction actions may be different from those of the impact reduction actions.

Risk actionee

A risk actionee is the individual assigned the implementation of a risk response action or actions to respond to a particular risk or set of risks. They support and take direction from the risk owner.

3.5.4 Activities

The Risk Register is a live document and must be maintained through all of the risk management steps and throughout the lifecycle of the organisational activity. To be of value it must be updated on a very regular basis and trend analysis should accompany updates of the register so that management can quickly discern if the picture is improving or deteriorating.

3.5.5 Relationship

It is sometimes worth including the activity objectives at the top of the register so that participants in the identification process do not lose sight of the fact that they should be identifying risks to the objectives. The Risk Register needs to include additional information from that described above if it is going to be used for quantitative analysis.

3.6 ISSUE LOG

3.6.1 Purpose

To capture and maintain information in a consistent, structured manner on all of the identified issues that have already occurred and require action. These issues may include risks that have materialised and have changed from possible events to actual events.

3.6.2 Background

Each organisation will need to decide on the precise content of its Issue Log. The layout of the log (typically reading from left to right) should reflect the sequence in which information is captured. The recognised purpose of the Issue Log is to collect sufficient information to enable a timely and appropriate response to be made to the events that have materialised. Issues may arise as a result of the occurrence of risks already documented in the Risk Register. The ability to transfer relevant information between the Risk Register and the Issue Log will enhance the effectiveness of management processes.

Like the Risk Register, for document management purposes, the Issue Log should carry a title (reflecting the organisational activity) date, date last updated, version number, author and file reference.

3.6.3 Composition

Typically an Issue Log will include as a minimum:

- Issue identifier
- Issue category — *strategic / prog / proj* *op*
- Issue description
- Impact
- Action required
- Date action to be implemented
- Date action implemented
- Issue owner
- Issue actionee.

3.6.4 Activities

There is more immediacy surrounding the contents of an Issue Log as it records events that have already occurred and in many instances require immediate attention. If a planning application for a new headquarters building has been rejected, if the regulator governing your industry has imposed a new pricing regime, or the government has imposed a windfall tax, all of these issues require immediate attention. There needs to be a clear understanding of the actual or potential scale of the impact, what needs to be done and in what order, what the timeframe is to be, the costs and which individuals will implement the response.

3.6.5 Relationship

The Issue Log must be coordinated with the Risk Register.

Management of risk process 4

4 Management of risk process

4.1 INTRODUCTION

This chapter describes the management of risk process. It is divided into four primary management of risk processes known as:

- Identify
- Assess
- Plan
- Implement.

Collectively these processes form a logical sequence of steps necessary for the adoption of a robust approach to the implementation of risk management. They are carried out in sequence, as any one step cannot be undertaken until the preceding step has been completed. They are all iterative in nature in that when additional information becomes available, it is often necessary to revisit earlier steps and carry them out again, to achieve the most informative result.

The overall management of risk process is illustrated in Figure 4.1. The steps are represented as a circle of arrows as it is common for the entire process to be completed several times in the lifecycle of an organisational activity.

The activity 'Communicate' deliberately stands alone as the findings of any individual step may be communicated to management for action prior to the completion of the overall process.

'Embed and Review' embraces all of the steps in the process as this activity looks at each individual step in turn to determine its contribution to the overall effectiveness of the complete process. The management of risk principles form the foundation for all risk management activities and permeate all risk management processes.

Figure 4.1 The management of risk process

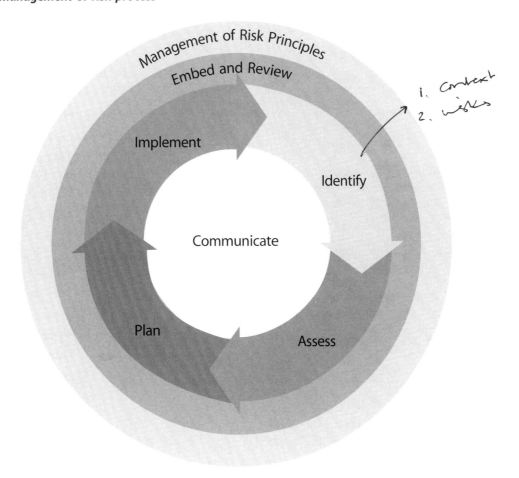

The M_o_R process is closely aligned to the Orange Book, referred to in the Introduction. Below is a diagrammatic comparison of the M_o_R process against the process included in the Orange Book. For simplicity and comparison purposes, the steps are expressed linearly. Keep in mind, however, that risk management is not composed of simple end-to-end steps, but is an iterative process.

The M_o_R process has made understanding and taking account of the context an explicit step within the Identify process to ensure that not only are the context activities undertaken, but undertaken at the right time in the overall process, and every time the risk management is updated on any organisational activity. Likewise, the M_o_R Assess process includes one step for estimating the probability and impact of individual risks and a separate step for evaluating the net effect of threats and opportunities when aggregated together. In addition 'Addressing Risks' and 'Reviewing and Reporting Risks' have been renamed to aid comprehension, communication and application of the activities required to complete these aspects of risk management and reflect other best practice guides.

Figure 4.2 Comparison of the steps within the M_o_R process and the Orange Book

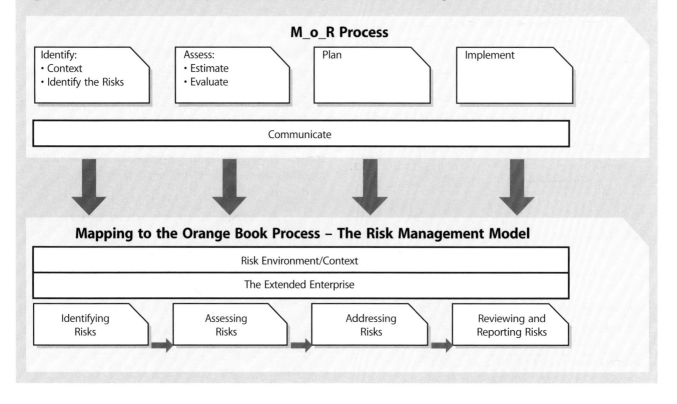

As risk management involves group participation, the overall process and its constituent incremental steps must be readily understood. Each of the steps is described in turn below, as an individual process.

The individual processes are described using their own unique goals, inputs, outputs, barriers, techniques and tasks. A simple process map for each step is included in Figure 4.3, which illustrates the four types of information movement. These types of data movement are used to describe how the management of risk steps are implemented and how the output of one process forms the input to the subsequent process. An explanation of the terminology used is as follows:

- **Process goals** are the key outcomes of the process. For instance, the process goals for the Identify step are to identify both the risks and opportunities facing the activity under examination as comprehensively as possible.

- **Process definition** is a graphical representation of the types of information movement.

- **Process inputs** describe the information that is transformed by the process. The absence of appropriate inputs may prohibit a process taking place. Partially completed inputs may enable a process to be completed but in many instances would require a process to be repeated when more complete information was available.

- **Process outputs** describe the information produced by the process, which will form the inputs to the subsequent process.

- **Process barriers** describe possible restrictions that may hinder the completion of a process. They are the same for each process.

- **Process techniques** describe the recognised risk management techniques that may be used to support the completion of the process. The techniques listed are described in more detail in Appendix B.

- **Process tasks** are the actions completed to transform the inputs into outputs, supported by the techniques and restricted by the barriers.

Figure 4.3 Process elements are by inputs, outputs, barriers and techniques

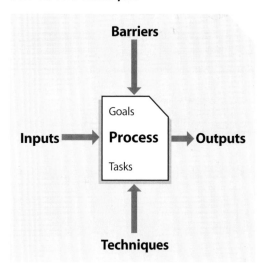

4.1.1 Common process barriers

As the barriers to the implementation of risk management are common to all the steps, they are described once here. Practitioners recognise that there are a series of barriers or constraints common to the implementation of all of the steps in the risk management process. Some of the barriers are described below:

- Lack of an organisational culture that appreciates the benefits of risk management
- Immature risk management practices
- Lack of risk facilitation resources and time
- Lack of policies, processes, strategies and plans
- Lack of a senior management risk champion
- Lack of training, knowledge and formal risk tools and techniques
- Lack of clear guidance for managers and staff
- Lack of incentivisation for the participation in risk management.

4.2 IDENTIFY – CONTEXT

4.2.1 Context goals

The primary process goal of the Context step within the Identify process is to obtain information about the planned activity. This will include understanding:

- What the activity objectives are
- What the scope of the activity is
- What assumptions have been made
- How complete the information is
- Who the stakeholders are and what their objectives are
- Where the activity fits in relation to the organisational structure
- The organisation's own environment (industry, markets, products and services etc.)
- The organisation's approach to risk management.

4.2.2 Context process definition

The Context process is described graphically in Figure 4.4.

4.2.3 Context inputs

The inputs for this step are the documents that are examined to gain an understanding of the activity being undertaken. The inputs must include sufficient information to provide, as a minimum, an understanding of the objectives, scope, timeframe, budget and participants. These are described in Table 4.1.

objectives / scope / timeframe / budget / participants

Figure 4.4 The Context process definition and information flows

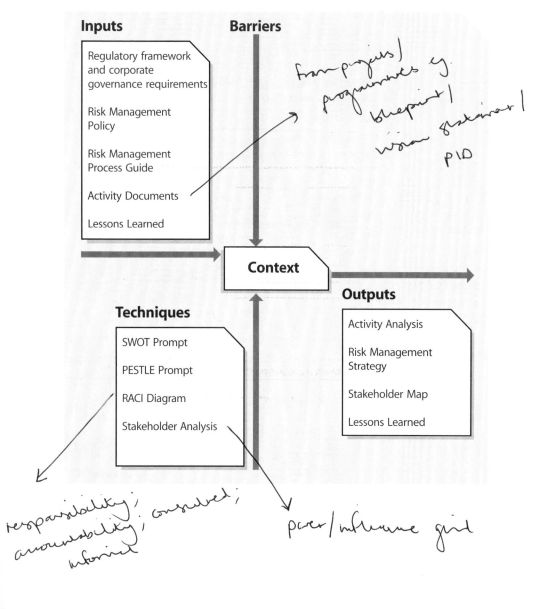

from projects / programmes eg. blueprint / vision statement / PID

responsibility; accountability; consulted; informed

power / influence grid

Table 4.1 Context inputs

Input	Explanation
Regulatory framework and corporate governance requirements	Depending on the activity under investigation it may be necessary to understand the organisation's regulatory framework and specific corporate governance requirements.
Risk Management Policy	The approach adopted for the Context step should reflect the Risk Management Policy and the required approach to management of risk, including recognition of the organisation's risk appetite. The approach should also accord with the principles to be used and the required approach to the allocation of accountability and responsibility for the management of risk across the organisation. Account should be taken of any instructions covering how risks are to be identified, assessed and controlled.
Risk Management Process Guide	Account should be taken of the process guide in terms of how the individual steps in the risk management process should be implemented.
Activity documents	The nature of the activities that will be studied as part of the Context step will be dictated by the type of activity under examination. Some of the common activities and their associated documents are described below.
	If the activity is setting *strategic direction* or evaluating a business plan, it is likely to involve examining as a minimum: the market, the number of competitors, barriers to entry, dominance of suppliers, the life expectancy of the market, projected income, costs of entry and time to market.
	If the activity is a *programme*, depending on its progress through the programme lifecycle, it is likely to involve examining the: programme objectives, stakeholders, interdependencies between the projects making up the programme, and the documents that would be examined for a project (see below). The latter would include the schedule and cost plan for example, but not necessarily the individual project details themselves, because of the possible volume of information.
	If the activity is a *project*, depending on its progress through the project lifecycle, it is likely to involve examining the: Project Initiation Document, project objectives, stakeholders, schedule, cost plan, organisational chart, plans, specifications, progress reports, external and internal approvals, change control process, stage gate/milestone process and contractual arrangements. In certain public sector projects, an additional input may be either an optimism bias calculation, conducted to support decision-making, an estimation of outturn costs prior to conducting a risk analysis, or a risk potential assessment used to estimate an activity's level of risk exposure at the beginning of the OGC Gateway Review Process.
	If the activity is a new or existing *operation*, it is likely to involve examining the: purpose of the operation, interfaces with other operations, the sequence of activities in the operation, stakeholders, use of information technology, the operational dependencies, equipment, man-machine interfaces and constraints.
Lessons learned	Depending on the type of activity being undertaken, it may be appropriate to seek out and examine any lessons learned reports available: these will describe events and activities that did not have a favourable outcome and, should they be repeated, may be potential sources of risk.

4.2.4 Context outputs

The results of this step form the inputs to the following step, Identify the risks. The contribution of the Context step in informing the process will be directly related to the thoroughness with which that step has been undertaken. A risk manager's ability to ask informed questions during the Identify the risks step will be influenced largely by knowledge of the planned activity gained during the Context step.

Table 4.2 Context outputs

Output	Explanation
Activity analysis	As a result of reviewing the planned activity it may be necessary to prepare a series of notes. For example, any assumptions made while interpreting the information examined should be recorded for verification in later steps. These notes will also describe to what degree the information is complete and the significance of any shortfalls.
Risk Management Strategy	Describes the goals of applying risk management to the activity, a description of the process that will be adopted, the roles and responsibilities, risk thresholds, the timing of risk management interventions, the deliverables, the tools and techniques that will be used and reporting requirements. It may also describe how the process will be coordinated with other management activities.
Stakeholder Map	Details should also be captured of stakeholders and an appropriate vehicle might be a Stakeholder Map. (A Stakeholder Map is a representation of stakeholders and their interests.) This is a simple diagrammatic representation of the stakeholders involved in an activity. It will also be useful to establish the degree of power and influence that stakeholders are anticipated to have over the life of the activity.
Lessons learned	Although they are not compiled during this step, lessons learned should feed into the Identify step and inform the identification of possible threats and opportunities.

4.2.5 Context barriers

See the common process barriers listed as part of the introduction to this chapter.

4.2.6 Context techniques

The list of risk management techniques included in Figure 4.4 is not exhaustive. It illustrates some of the most common techniques, namely:

- SWOT prompt
- PESTLE prompt
- RACI diagram
- Stakeholder analysis.

A SWOT prompt can be used as a reference during a workshop, when participants do not raise subjects that should be addressed.

A PESTLE prompt supports the identification of external political, economic, social, technological, legislative and environmental risk.

The use of a RACI diagram forces the documentation of the sequence of activities to be undertaken and which party will be responsible or accountable for each activity, and who will need to be consulted or informed.

Stakeholder analysis will help capture who the stakeholders are, their respective roles in the activity and their degree of participation. A stakeholder analysis can be used for complete organisations or parts of organisations, such as divisions or departments.

4.2.7 Context tasks

The process tasks will involve the examination of the activity information available. The information examined will vary according to the type of activity and whether it is strategic, programme, project or operation related. Typical tasks for the Context step are shown in Table 4.3.

Table 4.3 Context tasks

Activity objectives	Establish the objectives of the organisational activity under examination. This is the very first activity of the risk Context step. (This will allow the assessment criteria to be agreed and a probability impact grid to be compiled.) It will also be important to understand if the activity objectives reflect and are aligned with the organisation's objectives. (This should prevent the activity objectives being changed post-commencement of the risk identification process.)
Activity scope	Establish the primary components of the activity. Determine whether a map or flow chart of the organisational activity has been prepared to make explicit the activities and their interdependencies. (This will allow a risk breakdown structure to be prepared to understand the sources of risk.)
Assumptions	Understand the assumptions that have been made at this stage and how they would affect the activity if they proved to be incorrect.
Completeness of information	Discover what information exists, what is unavailable and how this reflects on the uncertainty of the activity.
Stakeholder analysis	It is important to understand how stakeholders are involved, the limits of their powers, their objectives and views and when they need to be engaged. Stakeholders generally include the activity sponsors, the participants, local or central government, end-user representatives and the community at large. It is important that the primary stakeholders' requirements have been incorporated in both the activity objectives and the activity brief and that they have 'signed-up' to the declared objectives. The primary stakeholders are defined here as those who can: withdraw funding, withhold approval, withdraw from participation (such as suppliers, contractors, designers or consultants), decline insurance, reject the end deliverable or stop the activity on health and safety or environmental grounds. A product of this task would be the preparation of a Stakeholder Map.
Internal context	Establish where the activity fits in relation to the organisational structure.
External context	Establish the organisation's own environment (industry, markets, products and services etc.). Determine whether the regulatory framework has been established and the reporting and audit requirements are known.
Approach to risk management	Establish if risk management has been sponsored and supported by senior management within the organisation. Determine if senior management have paved the way for risk management by communicating to the organisation the need for and benefits of risk management and the requirement to embed risk management throughout the organisation.
Risk Management Strategy	Whatever the activity relates to, it is recommended that a Risk Management Strategy is prepared. Information will be gleaned from the business plan, the activity objectives, the brief (or scope), the stakeholders (internal and external), the activity process, the budget, time schedule and the resources. Typical contents are described in Appendix A.
Lessons learned	Review lessons learned reports where available to understand the possible sources of risk.

4.3 IDENTIFY – IDENTIFY THE RISKS

4.3.1 Identify the risks goals

The primary goal of the Identify the risks step within the Identify process is to identify the risks to the organisation that would reduce or remove the likelihood of the organisation reaching its objectives while maximising the opportunities that could lead to improved performance. This will include:

- Identifying the threats and opportunities to the activity
- Preparing a Risk Register
- Preparing key performance indicators ╪ *tolerances*
- Understanding the stakeholders' view of the risks.

4.3.2 Identify the risks process definition

The Identify process is described graphically in Figure 4.5.

4.3.3 Identify the risks inputs

The inputs for this step are the documents that are examined to gain an understanding of the potential threats and opportunities and their individual characteristics (see Table 4.4).

Table 4.4 Identify the risks inputs

Input	Explanation
Activity analysis	The analysis was undertaken during the Context step and will be a primary source of information during this step.
Risk Management Strategy	The content of the strategy was discussed in the Context step.
Stakeholder Map	Created or updated during the Context step.
Lessons learned	Lessons learned from completed activities record what went well and should be repeated and what did not go well and should be improved on should a similar activity be embarked on in the future. Capturing lessons learned is essential for informed decision-making and business improvement to avoid the repetition of actions that had an unfavourable outcome and to capitalise on the positive outcomes.
Issues	These are matters that are identified and recorded as unresolved, in terms of the approach to be adopted. An issue may be removed or translated into a scope item, a fixed cost, or a risk.

Figure 4.5 The Identify the risks process definition and information flows

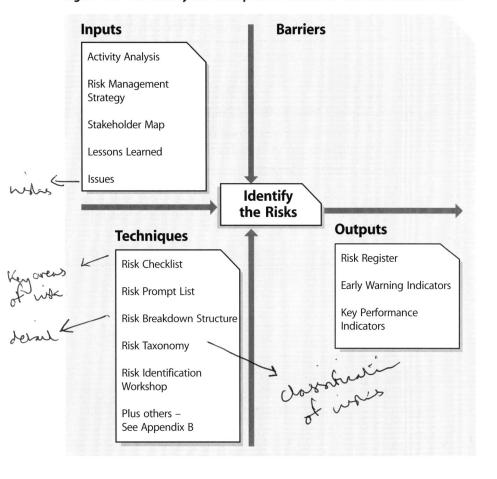

4.3.4 Identify the risks outputs

The outputs are the documents necessary to carry out the subsequent steps in the process (see Table 4.5). The key document is the Risk Register populated with the threats and opportunities.

Table 4.5 Identify the risks outputs

Output	Explanation
Risk Register	The content of the register needs to be tailored to the activity undertaken. The typical contents of a Risk Register are included in Appendix A. The risks detailed in the register should be structured using the section headings from the business case prepared for the activity, a risk breakdown structure, a risk taxonomy, or the stages in the project lifecycle. The benefit of structuring the risks in this way is to ensure that the risk identification process is comprehensive and there are no blind spots. When the first version of the Risk Register is produced, it will be obvious if certain areas of a project lifecycle (for instance) have not been addressed if no risks have been recorded against one or more phases. The Risk Register is a key communication tool as it is used and incrementally developed and updated throughout the entire management of risk process.
Early warning indicators	Early warning indicators may be sales figures, measures of liquidity, staff turnover, absenteeism and profit measured against turnover.
Key performance indicators	Key performance indicators may relate to organisational goals or performance against targets relating to a specific initiative such as penetrating a new market.

4.3.5 Identify the risks barriers

See the common process barriers listed as part of the introduction to this chapter.

4.3.6 Identify the risks techniques

The list of risk management techniques included in Figure 4.5 above is not exhaustive. It illustrates some of the most common techniques, namely:

- Risk checklist
- Risk prompt list
- Risk breakdown structure
- Risk taxonomy

- Risk identification workshop.

Risk checklists are useful aids in that they ensure that risks identified on previous similar activities are not overlooked for the current activity under examination.

Risk prompt lists commonly stimulate thinking about the sources of risk in the widest context through the provision of risk categories and sources of risk from within the organisation and in the external organisational environment.

Risk breakdown structures help clarify the potential sources of risk across operations, a project, a programme or an entire organisation. When used for an entire organisation, they can be organised to define the total extent of business operations required to accomplish the organisational activities.

Risk taxonomies, in a similar way to risk breakdown structures, provide a graphical representation of the sources of risk. They enable business activities to be disaggregated with threats and opportunities to be broken down into manageable components. This aids understanding, but also allows subsequent aggregation for exposure measurement, management, and reporting purposes.

Holding a risk identification workshop is one of the quickest methods of gaining a consensus among a group of activity participants regarding the threats and opportunities facing the activity. If there is sufficient time, consensus can also be obtained on the risk impacts and probabilities.

4.3.7 Identify the risks tasks

The process tasks will involve orchestrating the identification activities by involving the most appropriate participants in the right manner, after having prepared them for their role.

Typical tasks for the Identify the risks step are shown in Table 4.6.

Table 4.6 Identify the risks tasks

Task	Description
Analyse the context	Use the activity analysis output from the previous step to understand the background to the activity and the potential sources of risk.
Lessons learned	Review lessons learned reports, where available, to establish the risks that materialised on previous projects to understand potential threats to the activity under examination.
Participants	Establish and ask the most appropriate activity participants to take part in the risk identification process to ensure the approach is comprehensive and to avoid blind spots.
Risk breakdown structure	Prepare a risk breakdown structure or similar aid to support risk identification.
Risk checklists and risk prompt lists	Reference risk checklists or risk prompt lists to assist in the identification process.
Aim and benefits	Explain the aim and benefits of the M_o_R process as a whole to the participants to gain support for and increase participation in the process.
Cause, event and effect	Explain the difference between cause, event and effect to the participants, with the aid of examples. (This should reduce the number of instances where participants offer effects rather than risk events during the identification process.)
Identify the threats and opportunities	Carry out one-to-one interviews, workshops, questionnaires, meetings, brainstorming or nominal group activities to identify (in conjunction with the participants) the threats and opportunities facing the activity.
Gain a consensus	Gain a consensus among the participants as to the threats and opportunities.
Clarity	Take time to ensure that the threat and opportunity descriptions are as clear and full as possible so that when they are revisited at a later date, the meaning behind the descriptions is still understood. It is helpful to record the 'originator' of the risks so that if clarification is required at a later stage, they can be consulted about the description.
Record the information on a Risk Register	Ensure the information obtained during this process is captured on the Risk Register.
Structure the Risk Register	Structure the Risk Register using risk categories (risk group headings) such as political, economic, financial etc., to enable the register to be more easily read, digested and navigated.
Early warning indicators	Identify early warning indicators that can be used proactively to forewarn of adverse trends that can erode organisational performance.
Key performance indicators	Identify key performance indicators that will measure critical business systems.
Cost estimate	Obtain a copy of the cost estimate to support the Estimate step that follows.

4.4 ASSESS – ESTIMATE

4.4.1 Estimate goals

The primary goal of the Estimate step within the Assess process is to assess the threats and the opportunities to the organisation in terms of their probability and impact. The risk proximity will also be of interest to gauge how quickly the risk is likely to materialise if no action were taken. This will require an understanding of:

- The probability of the threats and opportunities in terms of how likely they are to occur
- The impact of each threat and opportunity in terms of the activity objectives. For example, if the objectives are measured in time and cost, the impact will be measured in units of time and cost
- The proximity of these risks and opportunities with regard to when they might materialise.

4.4.2 Estimate process definition

The Estimate process is described graphically in Figure 4.6.

4.4.3 Estimate inputs

The inputs to the Estimate step are the documents that will provide the information needed to allow probability and impact to be assessed as accurately as possible (see Table 4.7).

Table 4.7 Estimate inputs

Input	Explanation
Risk Register	The Risk Register at this stage will contain a log of the threats and opportunities identified. The risks will be listed under the categories to which they relate. Each risk will have been assigned a unique reference number for ease of discussion and communication. Where possible, the risk owner and risk actionee should have been identified.
Early warning indicators	As identified during the Identify step.
Key performance indicators	As identified during the Identify step.
Cost estimate and industry characteristics	Additional inputs to the management of risk process are likely to be the cost estimate and any specific industry characteristics such as the tender price index in the construction industry (to help sponsors understand if the annual increase in tender prices is higher or lower than the retail price index, for example).

Figure 4.6 The Estimate process definition and information flows

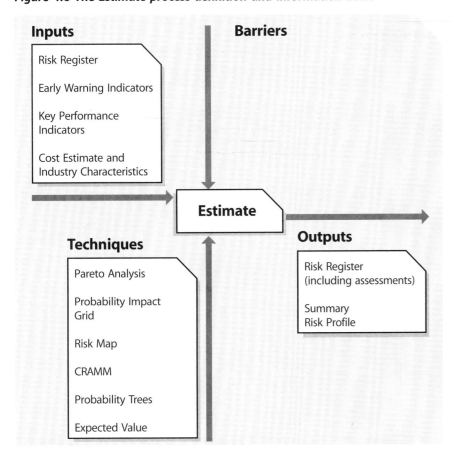

4.4.4 Estimate outputs

The outputs are the documents necessary to carry out the subsequent steps in the process, to complete the Evaluate step of the Assess process if it is appropriate to aggregate the risks and their impacts, and continue into the Plan step (see Table 4.8).

Table 4.8 Estimate outputs

Output	Explanation
Risk Register	The Risk Register is updated to include the probability of each threat and opportunity materialising and the impact of each threat and opportunity should they materialise. The very least that is required is to be able to distinguish between those events that will have a major impact on a business activity and those that will have a minor impact. This will enable risk management activity to be prioritised to achieve maximum effect.
Summary Risk Profile	This is a simple mechanism to increase visibility of risks. It is a graphical representation of the information found in the Risk Register.

4.4.5 Estimate barriers

See the common process barriers listed as part of the introduction to this chapter.

4.4.6 Estimate techniques

The list of risk management techniques included in Figure 4.6 is not exhaustive. It illustrates some of the most common techniques, namely:

- Pareto analysis
- Probability impact grid
- Risk map
- CRAMM
- Probability trees
- Expected value.

Pareto analysis is useful in focusing management effort on those risks that have the potential to have the greatest impact on a project or an organisation's objectives. Pareto analysis is the expression given to the simple process of ranking or ordering risks (by severity) once they have been assessed, to determine the order in which they should be managed. It is important to allocate resources to the significant few rather than the insignificant many.

Probability impact grids are essential for ensuring a consistent approach to risk analysis in terms of the assessment of probability and impact.

Risk maps are helpful in communicating, in the form of a simple grid, the range of severity of the risks identified (representing a combination of probability and impact).

CRAMM (the acronym for CCTA Risk Analysis and Management Method) is both a technique and a software tool. It is a very comprehensive aid for understanding information security risk and assessing, designing and managing the creation of an information security strategy. Its key benefits are that it already contains a list of assets to form an asset model, a schedule of threats and also a library of responses to the threats (called countermeasures).

Probability trees are useful in ensuring that a team has taken into account all of the possible outcomes of the range of solutions under examination. Diagrams are a helpful way of representing a situation as they enable the communication of ideas and options.

Most decision situations clearly have more than one outcome. When evaluating problems or situations where there is uncertainty about the outcome, the concept of expected values is particularly important. If it is possible to assign a probability to each outcome being achieved, the combination of the weighted outcomes can be calculated. The sum of the weighted outcomes is known as the expected monetary value.

4.4.7 Estimate tasks

The activities in the Estimate step are the tasks necessary to capture the likelihood of the identified threats and opportunities occurring and their impact, should they materialise, and also to record the results in the Risk Register. Some of these activities are shown in Table 4.9.

Table 4.9 Estimate tasks

Task	Description
Assessment	Prepare a probability impact grid to ensure a consistent approach is adopted for the assessment of likelihood and impact.
Description	Revisit the risk identification step if any of the threat or opportunity descriptions are insufficiently clear to be able to assess them, or they require rewording to reflect recent events.
Probability and impact	Assess the likelihood (probability) and impact of the threats and opportunities for each risk identified.
Risk proximity	Assess when the threat or opportunity is likely to materialise.
Risk relationships	Understand if the risks will occur sequentially (in series) or concurrently (in parallel).
Deciding what to model	Decide if very high impact, very low likelihood events should be modelled.
Document	Document the findings in the Risk Register.
Participants	Ensure personnel within the organisation with the appropriate knowledge and expertise are involved in the assessment process and that they are unbiased (that is, risk neutral – neither risk averse nor risk seeking – and are not seeking a particular result to suit their own ends).
Granularity of measures	Determine if there is sufficient granularity in the qualitative or quantitative assessment measures adopted to enable risks to be ranked and in turn to enable risk management activity to be prioritised.
Distributions	Select appropriate distributions to represent the risks such as triangular or uniform (where quantitative analysis techniques were deployed).
Clarification	Establish if the risk descriptions are clearly understood prior to estimation.
Consensus	Obtain a consensus on the estimates captured.
Ranking	If appropriate at this stage, having assessed the likelihood and impact, rank the risks in accordance with the estimated monetary value of each risk.

4.5 ASSESS – EVALUATE

4.5.1 Evaluate goals

The primary goal of the Evaluate step within the Assess process is to understand the net effect of the identified threats and opportunities on an activity when aggregated together. This may include preparing, for example, the following:

- An estimated monetary value (EMV) calculation, which records the weighted average of the anticipated impact.
- A risk model, which aggregates the risks together using a simulation technique.
- A net present value (NPV) calculation using an accepted discount rate.

4.5.2 Evaluate process definition

The Evaluate process is described graphically in Figure 4.7.

4.5.3 Evaluate inputs

The inputs for this step are the documents that are examined to gain an understanding of the activity being undertaken, principally generated in the Estimate step. These are described in Table 4.10.

Table 4.10 Evaluate inputs

Input	Explanation
Risk Register	During the previous step the register will have been updated with the probability and the impact of the threats and opportunities. The way the probability and impact will have been described will depend on whether the decision was made to use either qualitative or quantitative measures.
Summary Risk Profile	For details see the Estimate step.

Figure 4.7 The Evaluate process definition and information flows

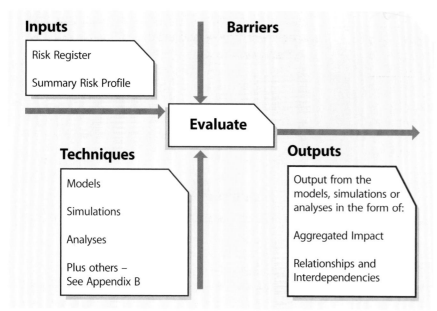

4.5.4 Evaluate outputs

The outputs are the documents and other information necessary to carry out the subsequent steps in the process (see Table 4.11).

Table 4.11 Evaluate outputs

Output	Explanation
Aggregated impact	Aggregation refers to the net effect of the threat and opportunity assessments when combined together.
	All outputs will be an aggregation of the threats and opportunities in some form. The specific outputs will be dictated by the objectives of the risk management study and may include: ■ Investment model results ■ Project quantitative costs risk analysis results ■ Project quantitative schedule risk analysis results ■ Scenario analysis ■ Sensitivity analysis ■ Simulation.
Relationships and interdependencies	The documents may also contain a description of the inter-relationship between specific threats and opportunities and what the strength of the correlation is thought to be.

4.5.5 Evaluate barriers

See the common process barriers listed as part of the introduction to this chapter.

4.5.6 Evaluate techniques

The list of risk management techniques included in Figure 4.7 is not exhaustive. It illustrates some of the most common techniques, namely:

■ Models
■ Simulations
■ Analyses.

Models are invaluable in that they enable relatively inexpensive representations of real-life situations to be created to discern optimum solutions, before any capital expenditure is made.

Simulations are helpful in generating and describing reliable confidence levels in achieving the activity objectives, commonly measured in cost and time. With the aid of contemporary software, simulations can be undertaken very quickly.

Analyses enable 'what if' scenarios to be carried out so that alternative strategies can be understood quickly and economically prior to decision-making.

4.5.7 Evaluate tasks

The activities in the Evaluate step are the tasks necessary to capture the right information to allow effective assessment of the relationships and interdependencies of the risks in their context. This assessment is crucial in the planning stage that follows. Some of these activities are shown in Table 4.12.

Table 4.12 Evaluate tasks

Task	Description
Simulation	If the decision is to adopt quantitative analysis based on the use of probability distributions to represent threats and opportunities, then it is more than likely that simulation techniques will be used to examine these events in combination. The two best-known simulation techniques are called Monte Carlo and Latin hypercube. A description of simulation and these two most widely adopted simulation techniques are described in Appendix B.
Risk relationships	Make an informed and well-reasoned assessment of the relationship between the risks (using influence diagrams where appropriate).
Correlation	Consider the merit of modelling the correlated risks in terms of whether the correlation is positive or negative and the strength of the correlation.
Sensitivity analysis	Carry out a 'what if' analysis to understand the significance of including or omitting particular risks.
Risk types	Take a conscious decision as to whether to omit very high impact, very low probability risks from the analysis due to their heavy distortion of the results. If this decision is taken, then these omissions must be recorded alongside the results.

4.6 PLAN

The primary goal of the Plan step is to prepare specific management responses to the threats and opportunities identified ideally to remove or reduce the threats and to maximise the opportunities. Attention to this step ensures as far as possible that the business and its staff are not taken by surprise if a risk materialises.

4.6.1 Plan process definition

The Plan process is described graphically in Figure 4.8.

4.6.2 Plan inputs

The inputs to the Plan step are the documents and other information from the previous process steps that will enable effective decision-making in planning responses to risks, whether they are threats to be removed or reduced, or opportunities to realise additional benefits (see Table 4.13).

Figure 4.8 The Plan process definition and information flows

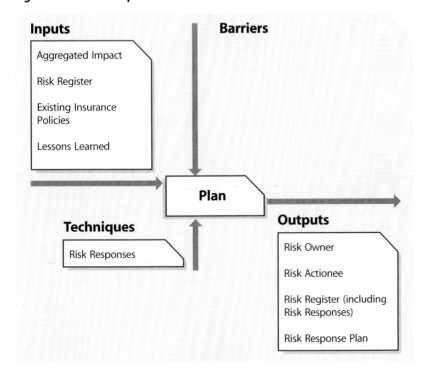

Table 4.13 Plan inputs

Input	Explanation
Aggregated impact	The extent of the aggregated impact may influence the choice of response categories.
Risk Register	Contains the information relating to the risks that have been identified and assessed.
Existing insurance policies	These may provide a means of responding to some of the risks identified.
Lessons learned	These may contain useful approaches for responding to some of the risks within the Risk Register.

4.6.3 Plan outputs

The outputs from the Plan step provide the information needed to take appropriate action in implementing the effective management of the risks identified and assessed in the previous steps of the M_o_R process. One of the most significant outputs is the identification of the individuals responsible for the response action and for overall ownership of each risk. Table 4.14 gives a brief description of these outputs.

Table 4.14 Plan outputs

Output	Explanation
Risk owner	Identification of the risk owner.
Risk actionee	Identification of the risk actionees.
Risk Register	To be updated with the chosen risk responses and the residual impact estimates.
	Risk responses contained within a Risk Register or recorded individually with each response on a separate page of a document will contain as a minimum the risk ID, risk category, risk description, risk status, the probability, impact in terms of cost and time, proximity (the date by which the actions are to be implemented), the response category, the risk owner, the risk actionee, actions to respond to the threat or opportunity (it is common for there to be multiple actions), the anticipated cost of the response and any secondary threats or opportunities that it is anticipated may arise from the response.
Risk Response Plan	It may be preferable to record the above information in a separate Risk Response Plan.

4.6.4 Plan barriers

See the common process barriers listed as part of the introduction to this chapter.

4.6.5 Plan tasks

The activities of the Plan process are the tasks identified to address risks or to maximise opportunities. Some of these activities are shown in Table 4.15.

Table 4.15 Plan tasks

Task	Description
Threat response category	Select a response for each of the risks from the categories: Removal, Reduction, Retention, Transfer or Share. These responses are described in Chapter 3, Table 3.7.
Opportunity response category	Select a response for each of the opportunities from the categories: Exploitation, Enhancement or Realisation. These responses are described in Chapter 3, Table 3.10.
Responses	Develop a risk response (or responses) for each threat and opportunity identified, both proactive and reactive.
Residual risk	Consider the residual probability and impact once the risk responses have been defined. (Refer to 'Risk Register' in section 4.6.3).
Balancing threat and response	Assess the cost of the proposed response against the cost of the risk should it materialise.
Balancing cost of capitalising on the opportunity against cost	Assess the cost of maximising an opportunity against the likelihood of realising the opportunity and the projected benefits.
Alternative responses	Develop alternative responses as appropriate, to permit selection of the most advantageous.
Organisational ownership	Identify the organisation that will retain ownership and accountability for the risks.
Risk owner	Identify the risk owner, the individual responsible for ensuring the planned response is implemented.
Risk actionee	Identify the risk actionee(s), the individual(s) responsible for implementing each of the response(s), having agreed the course of action, the cost and its timing with the risk owner.
Response reactions	Consider the emergence of secondary threats or opportunities through implementing proposed actions.
Timing	Determine when the responses will be implemented.
Domain knowledge	The most appropriate activity participant prepares each of the response actions.
Changing environment	Monitor changes to the environment as the magnitude of a threat or an opportunity and, therefore, the potential loss or gain, does not remain static.
Risk proximity	Consider the risk proximity and the required timing of responses.
Secondary risks	Be aware of secondary risks that may arise from initial response actions.

4.7 IMPLEMENT

The primary goal of the Implement step is to ensure that the planned risk management actions are implemented and monitored as to their effectiveness, and corrective action is taken where responses do not match expectations.

4.7.1 Implement process definition

The Implement process is described graphically in Figure 4.9.

4.7.2 Implement inputs

The inputs to the Implement step are the documents and other information from the previous process steps that will enable effective action to be taken to address the risks should they materialise, to realise potential opportunities, or to prevent threats occurring.

Table 4.16 Implement inputs

Input	Explanation
Risk owner	Identification of the risk owner.
Risk actionee	Identification of the risk actionee(s).
Risk Register	The primary input is the Risk Register, particularly if this document is being used to record not only the threats and opportunities and their assessment, but also the threat and opportunity response actions. If a risk database has been used then the files on the database will also form a core input.
Risk Response Plan	If the risk responses are recorded in a separate plan.

4.7.3 Implement outputs

The outputs of the Implement step are the documents and other information that enable effective monitoring and review of the management of risk activities, including financial impacts and new risks that may emerge as a result of actions taken or other factors (see Table 4.17).

Table 4.17 Implement outputs

Output	Explanation
Risk Progress Reports	The key outputs will be progress reports providing details of a combination of or all of the following:
	■ Progress of planned risk management actions
	■ Effectiveness of implemented actions
	■ Trend analysis of closed and new risks
	■ Insurance requirements
	■ Spend against contingencies
	■ Spend against response action budgets
	■ Numbers of risks emerging in the different risk categories
	■ Movement of risk against the key performance indicators
	■ Anticipated emerging risks that will require specific management attention.

4.7.4 Implement barriers

See the common process barriers listed as part of the introduction to this chapter.

Figure 4.9 The Implement process definition and information flows

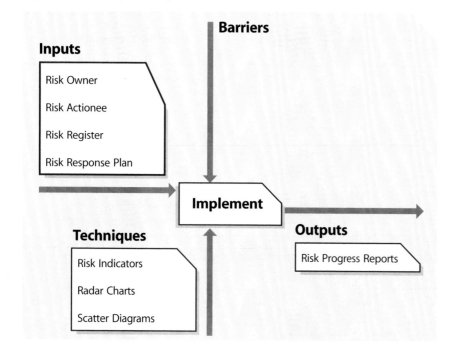

4.7.5 Implement techniques

The list of risk management techniques included in Figure 4.9 above is not exhaustive. It illustrates some of the most common techniques, namely:

- Risk indicators
- Radar charts
- Scatter diagrams.

Risk indicators are thresholds to describe acceptable levels of risk and can be used to illustrate whether post-assessment, the activity risks exceed or fall below the threshold.

Radar charts provide a visual representation of information in such a way that it can be readily digested. They are very appropriate for high-level dashboard reports that are intended to convey the highlights of a risk assessment.

Scatter diagrams, in a similar way to risk maps, can be used to represent pictorially the concentrations of risk (measured by probability and impact) to illustrate the degree of risk exposure for a particular activity or business area.

4.7.6 Implement tasks

The activities of the Implement step are the tasks designed to ensure that the planned responses have actually been implemented, that their effectiveness is monitored, and that action is taken to address risk actions that have not been effective or where a previously unidentified risk has materialised that requires immediate management attention. The three key actions are executing, monitoring and controlling.

Table 4.18 Implement tasks

Task	Description
Executing	The time, energy, effort and finances expended in the preceding steps will largely be wasted unless the planned responses are implemented. The implement step must ensure planned responses are implemented.
Monitoring	Monitoring is required to understand if the responses being implemented are effective in accomplishing the desired aim. Although monitoring is valuable, it is just a process of observation. It is neutral as it is outside of the activity taking place. Monitoring must be broader than simply reviewing action plans. It must also involve looking at emerging threat and opportunity.
Controlling	Unlike monitoring, controlling is not a neutral activity but requires intervention. Controlling uses the information collected during monitoring to take proactive action. To be effective, these actions must be economical, meaningful, appropriate, congruent (appropriate degrees of accuracy to suit the circumstances), timely, simple and operational.
Response actions	The Implement task includes assessing whether risk owners and risk actionees are implementing the threat and opportunity responses for which they are responsible.
Risk Register	The Risk Register must be kept up-to-date with new risks, closed risks, revised post-mitigation residual risk figures, planned responses, the individuals carrying out the roles of risk actionee and risk owner, sources of risk, the ramifications of entering into new contracts and threat and opportunity likelihoods.
Early warning indicators	Early warning indicators must be amended to reflect changes in the marketplace.
Horizon scanning	Time must be invested in looking at the emergence of new threats and opportunities.
Reporting	Reports should be provided on a regular cycle providing visibility of the progress being made in terms of mitigating, transferring or removing threats and maximising opportunities.

4.8 COMMUNICATE

Rather than being a distinct stage in the management of risk process, communication is an activity that is carried out throughout the whole process. A number of aspects of communication should be recognised and addressed if risk management is to be effective.

An organisation's exposure to risk is never static: effective communication is key to the identification of new threats and opportunities or changes in existing risks. Horizon scanning in particular depends on the maintenance of a good communications network, including relevant contacts and sources of information to facilitate the identification of changes that may affect the organisation's overall risk exposure.

The implementation of risk management is dependent on participation, and participation, in turn, is dependent on communication. It is important for management to engage with staff across the organisation to ensure that:

- Everyone understands the organisation's risk appetite, risk policy, risk process, risk strategies and regulatory requirements, in a way that is appropriate to their role. If this is not achieved, effective and consistent embedding of risk management will not be realised and risk priorities may not be addressed.

- Everyone understands the benefits of effective risk management and the potential implications if it is not done or is done badly.

- Each level of management, including the board, actively seeks and receives appropriate and regular assurance about the management of risk within their control. Effective communication provides assurance that risk is being managed within the expressed risk appetite and that risks exceeding tolerance levels are being escalated to pre-agreed levels of management.

- The procurement team understands the requirement for making risk ownership explicit within contracts and service level agreements. A lack of appreciation of the risk ownership split with a contracted party can invalidate the economic case for a project, contract or investment.

- Transferable lessons learned are communicated – as part of an enterprise-wide approach to risk management – to those who can benefit from them. For example, if one part of the organisation encounters a new risk and devises an effective control to deal with it, that lesson should be communicated to all other departments that may also encounter the same risk.

- There is no misunderstanding over the respective risk priorities within and across each business perspective. This will help management to avoid being diverted from the most significant risks and will enable appropriate levels of control to be applied to specific risks across the organisation.

- Any organisation providing outsourcing services has adequate risk management skills and processes. Gaining assurance that a partner organisation has implemented adequate risk management for itself will avoid dependence on a third party that may fail to deliver in an acceptable way, or may not deliver at all. The failure of contracted providers can disrupt critical business systems, which in turn can lead to a fall in shareholder confidence, damage to an organisation's reputation, and a decrease in share value, and has also been known to attract hostile takeover bids in some instances.

Risk management is also directly dependent on communication to provide assurance to third parties such as regulators, shareholders, stakeholders and staff that risks are being appropriately identified, assessed and controlled. The mediums for this communication are the annual review, statements of internal control and reports on planned activities such as investments, acquisitions and product development.

The typical contents of a Communications Plan are included in Appendix A.

Embedding and reviewing management of risk

5

5 Embedding and reviewing management of risk

5.1 INTRODUCTION

The purpose of this chapter is to introduce the need for the integration of risk management into the culture of the organisation, to explain how this can be achieved, and to highlight the need for regular reviews to ensure risk management is being appropriately and successfully handled across the organisation.

How an organisation manages its risk demonstrates a part of that organisation's core values and improves stakeholder confidence in the organisation's ability to cope with and manage its risks. The organisation therefore needs to ensure that risk management has been integrated successfully, has the necessary support, is addressed in an appropriate way and is successful. A key component of the management of risk integration within an organisation is the cultural acceptance and change required to embed management of risk principles and values within the organisation. This can be best achieved through a structured programme of activities that lead to the achievement of risk knowledge, understanding and education within the organisation.

Often smaller organisations can achieve better results, more quickly. Quite often the same individual undertakes multiple roles and has several responsibilities associated with the management of risk, which can result in a better understanding and quicker decision making. Also, within a small organisation, a smaller number of participants are typically involved overall. Within large organisations, on the other hand, the management of risk roles and responsibilities can be dispersed, resulting in a need for more complex integration and communication of the management of risk.

Ensuring that the appropriate decentralised or integrated management of risk roles and responsibilities are correctly identified and implemented for the organisation is key to the success of management of risk within that organisation.

The Managing Successful Programmes (MSP) publication provides detailed guidance on structuring and managing a programme of activities. Input to this programme could come from the methods and techniques described in this chapter (and elsewhere within this book), or from specific methods and techniques already in use within the organisation to embed other disciplines such as security awareness. In constructing such a programme, particular attention should be paid to identifying and describing the benefits that need to be realised, in advance of implementing the programme. This is because benefits management should be a continuous thread throughout the programme and regular assessments must be made to determine whether these benefits are being delivered as part of the programme.

An organisation needs to be able to measure the effectiveness and appropriateness of risk management, including the organisation's progress in embedding management of risk, and also its ability to develop its management of risk capability and maturity. The latter can be assessed using the maturity model described in Appendix D. The appropriateness of risk management within the organisation can be assessed against the organisation's known and communicated risk appetite. For specific risks this appetite is likely to be defined in terms of impact and frequency, whereas at an operational level it may be more practical to define the appetite in terms of value to be lost (or not gained), the impact on reputation, non-compliance (legal, regulatory, contractual, etc.) or the level of disruption or delay to operational activities.

One way of gauging the effectiveness of the risk management culture is the level by which risk management sponsorship and leadership is demonstrated and supported by senior management, in the way they own and lead on risk activities. There are other indicators that demonstrate how successfully and effectively the management of risk culture has been embedded. These include:

- The understanding of risk management policies and benefits by all staff
- The existence and operation of a transparent and repeatable risk management framework
- The support by the organisational culture of well thought-through risk taking and innovation
- The close linking of management of risk with the achievement of objectives
- The explicit assessment and management of the risks associated with working with partners

- The active monitoring and regular review of risks on a constructive 'no-blame' basis
- The sharing of examples and lessons learned across the company to better understand decision-making, benefits, improvements and pitfalls
- The reporting of risks to management in a timely manner (together with sufficient information to enable risk treatments to be developed) and the escalation of risks within appropriate timescales if they develop.

One aim of an organisation's risk practices is to embed a risk culture in which risk management is an integral and natural activity in the principles and ethos adopted by all staff within the organisation. This cannot and will not be achieved overnight. It will require a long-term goal with a clear, achievable plan to introduce risk management and, where necessary, change the mindset of individuals through an agreed strategy that fits with the culture of the organisation.

Changes in the tangible aspects of risk management (policy, processes, strategies, response plans, etc.) can typically be achieved relatively quickly and easily. The intangible aspects of embedding risk management into business processes can take up to a couple of years and establishing a full risk management culture can take several years to achieve.

It is important to ensure that the tone of and the cultural approach to the risk awareness programme fit in with the ethos of the company. Once an approach has been agreed, a Risk Improvement Plan should be developed (with key dates and targets) and implemented.

Reviewing management of risk, its capability, maturity, success and its integration should be part of an ongoing monitoring and management process. This should include regular assessments of maturity and capability, ongoing healthchecks and reviews of management of risk procedures and practices. Independent reviews (such as internal audit) should also be conducted to provide impartial observations to help improve management of risk activities and develop maturity or to verify findings and reviews.

5.2 MEASURING THE BENEFITS AND SUCCESS

When an organisation implements or develops its risk management capability, the organisation should measure this development, the benefits it brings to the organisation, and therefore its success.

The benefits to be achieved from the embedding programme should be clearly defined and documented at the start of the programme. These can then be assessed throughout the programme's implementation to ensure they are delivered. The Managing Successful Programmes publication describes in detail the benefits management process, including identifying benefits, quantifying benefits and the realisation of benefits. Areas where benefits may be identified or realised include:

- The organisation's ability to fulfil policies or legal requirements
- An improvement in the organisation's quality of service
- Internal operational improvements (such as improved decision-making process or more motivated workforce)
- An improved ability to respond to change (for example reducing costs by implementing changes more quickly)
- Increased revenue or reduced costs, while maintaining quality
- More informed decision-making capability.

A selection of methods that can be used to measure the positive effect of a risk culture follows. These assessment methods are closely aligned and linked to the collection and collation of information on the risk management principles and are part of the healthcheck that can be conducted in order to assess the level of maturity achieved:

- Questionnaires can be used to ask questions relating to the organisation, its business, people and activities. They can be issued in paper form during awareness courses or workshops to gauge how much has been absorbed; they can be issued electronically via email to gauge ad hoc levels of awareness, perhaps relating to a particular element of risk promotion that has been undertaken; or they can be made available through an intranet or at the end of a computer-based training (CBT) course for participants to complete online.
- Benchmarks can be used to measure the impact a risk management awareness programme has in an organisation, or the level of impact that introducing fresh or new risk management practices has. In order to establish a benchmark, a baseline should first be established. This defines the existing level of knowledge or practice, and therefore enables the difference (the impact of the activity) to be measured against the benchmark state.
- Everything within an organisation has a cost (either in terms of a monetary value or a time value) and therefore benefit should be measured, thereby measuring a return on the value/cost deployed. The simplest way of measuring benefits from an education,

training or awareness programme is through sampling understanding and knowledge within the staff via questionnaires.

■ The degree to which risk management has been integrated within the culture of the organisation provides a degree of measurement, for example integrated risk discussions and considerations within project, programme or management meetings.

■ The freedom, detail and speed with which risks are identified and reported to the correct people and then recorded, assessed and controlled provides a measurement on the improvement risk management has had to the organisation.

■ Risks can be managed more quickly and more effectively if individuals are able to make and understand their risk-based decisions more easily as a result of the knowledge and information collected or provided as part of the risk reporting process.

■ A risk-aware culture enables preventive and proactive views and decisions to be made, identifying risks as part of a risk informed decision-making process. This enables organisations to make better, more appropriate decisions.

5.3 SUCCESS FACTORS

There are a number of essential elements to identify when measuring success, which will probably be different for each organisation. The preferred methods for measuring success in implementing risk management practices and developing a risk management culture within an organisation are defined in Appendix C. The level to which these have been implemented and are successful can then be measured using the models reviewed in Appendix D.

Rather than discuss general success factors in detail, each organisation should identify specific success factors for themselves at the outset of the management of risk programme and define these as measurable benefits that can then be monitored and managed as part of the benefits management activities within the programme management practice (see the MSP publication).

High-level success factors include:

■ Visible sponsorship, endorsement and support from senior management

■ A defined and communicated Risk Management Policy

■ Regular communication on risk management within the organisation

■ Inclusion of risk management and its application within the induction programme

■ Inclusion of risk management and a review of key risks on the board agenda

■ Individual business unit Risk Registers and a consolidated organisation-wide Risk Register

■ An appointed board member responsible for risk management

■ Regular presentations on key risks and progress on the risk treatment plan to the internal audit committee

■ A clearly defined risk management process

■ Evidence of regular risk management communication

■ Inclusion of risk management responsibilities in job descriptions and personal objectives

■ Improved risk management understanding and knowledge within the organisation

■ Benchmarking of risk management awareness

■ Regular reviews/questionnaires to gauge risk management awareness.

5.4 SENIOR MANAGEMENT COMMITMENT AND SUPPORT

The responsibility for understanding and managing risk rests at board level. Processes for managing risk may be delegated to others to implement, but accountability remains with the nominated person at board level. Therefore, a clear demonstration of sponsorship, responsibility and endorsement from that board person is necessary to ensure that risk management is taken seriously, given the priority it deserves and embraced within the organisation.

The board has ultimate responsibility for risk management and relies on others, such as senior management and middle management, for:

■ The creation of a risk framework

■ The creation of a management infrastructure to ensure that risk is managed across the whole business (this may include the risk management function, the project/programme executive, senior management and the internal audit committee)

■ The inclusion of risk management in job descriptions, the setting of performance objectives aligned to the framework and the inclusion of risk in the appraisals process.

Useful methods for obtaining and developing senior management commitment and support include:

■ Having a board-level sponsor defined and communicated to all staff

■ Having risk responsibility clearly defined at board and senior management level

- Having risk delivery linked to performance objectives and performance reviews
- Ensuring that risk is discussed and emphasised in management meetings and cascaded to staff via appropriate communication methods (e.g. staff briefings, intranet, email and memos)
- Providing regular meetings, briefings or reports on risk to senior management that identify not only the risks, but also their potential impact in business terms
- Communicating and emphasising risk management successes and improvements
- Agreeing the internal controls for risk management with internal and external audit
- Ensuring that regular reporting on risk status is provided to the independent committees (such as the audit committee)
- Ensuring the risk management function has a direct reporting line to a senior executive.

5.5 BUILDING AND DEVELOPING AWARENESS

There is a need to develop, build and implement awareness of the risk management approach, activities, processes, responsibilities and techniques within the organisation in order to ensure the following:

- Risk identification occurs at all levels within the organisation
- Risks are reported and escalated in a timely manner
- Risks are assessed consistently across the organisation
- Risks are treated in an acceptable and appropriate way
- Opportunities from risk identification are understood, communicated and acted on
- A continual improvement process takes effect to ensure the same risks do not occur repeatedly.

A number of useful methods can be used to help build and develop risk awareness within an organisation. These include:

- Risk management champions (whereby individuals are identified in each area of the business to promote good risk management practice as part of their day-to-day role)
- The inclusion of risk responsibilities and activities in job descriptions, objectives and staff appraisals
- Delivering information on risk management as part of new staff inductions (this will help ensure new staff understand the importance of risk management, how

risks are identified, assessed and controlled, the role and responsibility that every person has within the organisation, and the actions expected of them)

- Having dedicated space on the organisation's intranet for risk management (this can include guidance to all staff on roles and responsibilities, what to do when a risk is identified, the method of risk assessment, how to record a risk, how to escalate a risk, and templates to download)
- Publishing and communicating risk-related articles that are mentioned in the news or in newspapers (these could be news stories about risk incidents and their consequences, or they could relate to good management practice and standards)
- The use of marketing products/tools to deliver a message or promote risk management (this could include developing a logo or particular phrase to support an awareness programme and using it on marketing products such as mouse mats, coasters, calendars, posters, foam balls).

5.6 IDENTIFYING AND ESTABLISHING OPPORTUNITIES FOR CHANGE

Organisations should identify opportunities to emphasise their support and commitment to risk management, deliver key messages, and check that risk management is taking place appropriately.

Trigger points should also be used to monitor and review risks and decisions made on those risks, thereby establishing a continual cycle of monitoring, review and update/improvement. This lifecycle for risk management ensures that risk-based decisions remain appropriate and informed as the organisation changes or its objectives change.

A selection of trigger points are discussed below:

- When organisations undertake or undergo changes in their organisational structure and/or personnel changes occur within that organisational structure. This establishes an opportunity to review and discuss the role of risk management within that structure, identify roles and responsibilities, and ensure that risk management is effectively defined and discharged with the new management team. It is also an ideal opportunity to discuss how good risk management can help the new management team achieve its objectives by reducing the incidence of failure, improved management, and a better understanding of risk.

■ Change management activities within the organisation provide suitable opportunities to identify, assess and record risks as part of that change process. They can also help develop an awareness of risk management and communicate the defined risk management processes, activities and guidance across the organisation so that these can be used as part of the management of change programme. Informed decisions can then be made taking into account the potential risks associated with certain decisions.

■ When new or changed standards are introduced into an organisation, these invariably involve amendment to processes. Adopting and communicating the risk management activities as part of these changes and the adoption of standards is vital to the successful understanding and acceptance of risk management.

■ Whenever something unexpected occurs or fails within an organisation, the organisation's risk management process can be used to assess the potential risk of that failure to the organisation. It also presents an ideal opportunity to improve the process and provide feedback or input into a lessons learned cycle to further develop and improve the risk approach and application. As part of the risk management process, understanding the failure, crisis or event, assessing it, and identifying a way of improving it, is accepted and expected practice within an organisation that has a good embedded risk management culture and discipline. Using a 'wash-up' or post-incident review meeting to conduct this activity and perform a review of any remaining risks demonstrates the existence of a continual improvement process and helps to reinforce the benefits that can be achieved through an embedded risk management culture.

5.7 MODIFYING BEHAVIOUR TOWARDS RISK MANAGEMENT

Organisations introducing risk management or developing their existing risk management practices will need to modify the behaviour and attitude of staff towards risk. This includes identifying, assessing and controlling risk. The resultant behaviour should fully support the risk management process.

In order to achieve this, the organisation will need to address the relevance of risk management to individuals and the organisation. This will include items such as:

■ If staff believe that it's not part of their job to be part of the risk management activities, the organisation will need to integrate risk management into job descriptions and objectives and communicate this to staff. This communication will need to explain the value link between the individual's risk management actions and behaviour and the overall impact. For example, a better performance appraisal means improved company performance, leading to greater job stability, better bonuses, etc.

■ By directly linking good risk management techniques and activities to an individual's performance rating, the organisation will have a greater degree of control and success in the application of those techniques and activities. This links back to the previous point – and one of the key motivational factors of staff in any organisation: personal success and benefit/recognition.

■ Integrating risk management into processes. An increasing number of processes include elements of risk management, whether they are projects, programmes (e.g. PRINCE2 or MSP), related processes or management processes (e.g. ITIL). Elements can include risk assessment, Risk Registers, risk responses, monitoring and reporting/escalating of risk. These are all important activities. However, risk management also needs to be embedded into the business processes so that it becomes an integrated element of business activity rather than an optional extra.

5.8 ROLES AND RESPONSIBILITIES

Table 5.1 summarises the roles and responsibilities of those who should be involved in developing and embedding the management of risk culture into the organisation, and reviewing management of risk within the organisation. The exact name for each role may vary. The level of resources applied to each role will also vary according to the size of the organisation.

Table 5.1 Roles and responsibilities

Role	Responsibilities
Accounting Officer (Chief Executive Officer)	■ Acts as the figurehead for the management of risk within the organisation.
Risk improvement manager (public sector) or risk manager (private sector)	■ Ensures the M_o_R framework is implemented ■ Carries out ongoing management of risk maturity assessments ■ Develops plans to improve management of risk ■ Develops management of risk guidance and training ■ Identifies lessons learned and disseminates learning ■ Undertakes risk management training and holds seminars to embed risk management ■ Develops a programme for the embedding of management of risk.
Programme, project and operational unit boards, senior responsible owners	■ Understand the M_o_R framework and their accountabilities ■ Implement the M_o_R framework within their areas of responsibility ■ Escalate programme, project and operational risks according to the strategic perspectives defined in the M_o_R framework ■ Promote management of risk principles ■ Manage the risk associated with programmes, projects and operational areas.
Risk specialists	■ Prepare strategic Risk Management Strategies including education, training, awareness and cultural embedding plans ■ Undertake qualitative and quantitative analysis with management ■ Prepare risk management reports.
Internal audit department	■ Makes formal assessments of management of risk implementation (e.g. Appendix C or the Treasury's Risk Management Assessment Framework) in areas of concern ■ Assesses the controls in place to manage, mitigate or reduce risks.
Managers across the organisation	■ Review and manage risk controls within their area of responsibility within the organisation ■ Promote management of risk and its principles to their staff.
All staff	■ Help identify and report or escalate risks to management.

Perspectives

6

6 Perspectives

6.1 INTRODUCTION

In the previous chapters, the principles, approach and generic process for undertaking risk management have been described. The way in which these principles, approach and processes are applied will vary according to the nature of the context within which they are being undertaken.

Within any organisation, the various contexts will lie somewhere on a continuum between:

- Maintaining the status quo through day-to-day management of the organisation's product or service delivery, and
- Establishing the future direction for the organisation and moving the organisation in that direction by means of change management.

Within this guidance, the various contexts will be described from different organisational perspectives. The organisational perspectives considered can be briefly described as:

- **Strategic** – concerned with ensuring overall business success, vitality and viability
- **Programme** – concerned with transforming business strategy into new ways of working that deliver measurable benefits to the organisation
- **Project** – concerned with delivering defined outputs to an appropriate level of quality within agreed time, cost and scope constraints
- **Operational** – concerned with maintaining appropriate levels of business services to existing and new customers.

6.1.1 Strategic

- Sets the scene for the management of risk across the entire organisation.
- Information flows need to be established between those with strategic responsibilities and those with operational and programme responsibilities.
- It would also be appropriate to establish information flows with those with project responsibilities where the project outputs are of strategic importance.

6.1.2 Programme

- Sets the scene for the management of risk within the programme and the projects that form part of the programme
- Further information flows need to be established between those with programme responsibilities and those with project responsibilities within the programme
- It would also be appropriate to establish information flows with those with operational responsibilities where the programme will have an impact on these.

6.1.3 Project

- Sets the scene for the management of risk within the project
- The nature of the information flows will depend on whether the project supports strategic, programme or operational objectives or a combination of these.

6.1.4 Operational

- Sets the scene for the management of risk within particular operational (service delivery) areas
- Further information flows need to be established between those with operational responsibilities and those with strategic, programme and project responsibilities where these will have an impact on the operational area.

Although these perspectives are described individually, there are important relationships that need to be established and maintained between these organisational perspectives for risk management to be effective. The inter-relationships between these perspectives can be shown diagrammatically in Figure 6.1.

Figure 6.1 Inter-relationships between different organisational perspectives

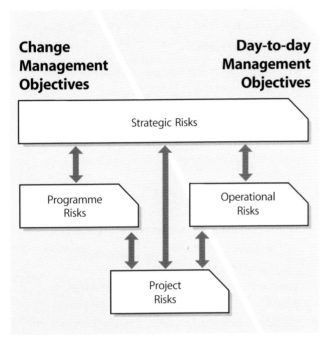

The purpose of the remainder of this chapter is to describe the application of management of risk from the strategic, programme, project and operational perspectives. Accordingly, each of the principles is described as outlined in Table 6.1.

Other perspectives could have been considered, such as:

- Business continuity
- Incident (crisis) management
- Health and safety
- Security

- Financial.

However, these are considered to be risk management specialisms in this guidance and are described briefly in Appendix E.

6.2 STRATEGIC PERSPECTIVE

6.2.1 Organisational context

The strategic perspective maintains a view of executive-level decision-making relative to the organisation's external environment and to other organisations that work with or against it.

Strategic risks are those risks concerned with ensuring overall business success, vitality and viability. Materialisation of a strategic risk will be perceivable externally by owners, investors or funders, and will affect the reputation of the organisation.

Strategic opportunities and threats are generally identified:

- Through escalation of risks from programme, project, or operational activities
- As a by-product of corporate and business planning activities
- By partner organisations that share interests with the organisation.

Strategic management considers all aspects of the organisation but pays particular attention to the value creating ability of a relatively few core services and capabilities of the organisation. It plays a vital role in broadly allocating resources to ventures and operational areas according to their relative risk and value to the

Table 6.1 Use of M_o_R principles to describe perspectives

Organisational context	Provides a brief description of the context of the perspective and identifies likely areas of uncertainty.
Nature of objectives	Describes the typical types of objectives set for the perspective.
Stakeholder involvement	Discusses the type and range of stakeholders that will be interested in or affected by the perspective.
M_o_R approach	Suggests how the approach to risk management may need to be adapted for the perspective in question.
Reporting	Identifies the need for reports from and to the perspective.
Roles and responsibilities	Lists the main roles that will have responsibility for risk management within the perspective and describes areas of responsibility.
Support structure	Discusses how risk management can be supported within the perspective.
Early warning indicators	Identifies the main type of early warning indicators relevant to the perspective.
Review cycle	Suggests how risk management processes should relate to the lifecycle of organisational activity relevant to the perspective.

organisation. In addition, it is responsible for managing the gaps that exist between programme, project and operational management. As a result, it makes structural changes from time to time as a way of affecting where gaps exist. Strategic management is exclusively responsible for positioning the organisation, initiating strategic change affecting capital (e.g. divestment, merger, acquisition and public sector equivalents), establishing investment priorities and overseeing business planning.

Emergent management approaches related to strategic risk management are portfolio management and enterprise-risk management (ERM). Both of these approaches help create an organisational view of risk and address associated management complexities.

Typical areas of uncertainty within the strategic perspective include:

- Additional or fewer participants in the organisation's operating space (e.g. new entrants)
- The reconfiguring of existing organisations (e.g. merger) providing a particular service or function that is relevant to the organisation (e.g. suppliers)
- Stakeholder (shareholder) perceptions of key policies, services or operational activities that would affect organisational reputation
- Changes to legislation or regulation that affect the core business or have a larger financial impact
- Changes in macroeconomic factors such as interest rates, inflation or exchange rates
- Political and market factors affecting the attractiveness or appropriateness of corporate services
- The emergence of new technologies that change the business model or public (consumer) expectations
- Significant threats to the life and well-being of large numbers of staff such as a pandemic influenza
- Fire, flood, building subsidence, acts of terrorism or other damage to key resources or core assets.

6.2.2 Nature of objectives

The strategic perspective is principally concerned with achieving desired outcomes by defending or changing organisational performance. Strategic objectives will generally consist of a mixture of the following types of objectives:

- **Financial:** these relate to tangible measures that satisfy stakeholder or shareholder expectations.
- **Core service:** these tend to relate to increasing efficiency, quality or output.

- **Stakeholder or customer:** these relate to ensuring that reputation is managed and demand for services remains strong and predictable.
- **Organisational capability:** these relate to ensuring that the organisation remains relevant and able to meet future needs (e.g. innovation and new service development).
- **Resource:** these relate to ensuring that staff and suppliers are providing the skills and commodities required by the organisation.

6.2.3 Stakeholder involvement

Strategic stakeholders are likely to include those drawn from the following groups:

- Owners or shareholders, investors or funders
- Key customers or customer groups
- Political, legal or regulatory bodies
- The wider community in which the affected organisation exists, such as the general public
- Strategic partners or suppliers
- Employees.

6.2.4 Management of risk approach

Risk management for the strategic perspective should be shaped by the Risk Management Policy, strategic Risk Management Strategy, and the Risk Management Process Guide.

The Risk Management Strategy for the strategic perspective will define how management of risk will be handled by the Accounting Officer/Chief Executive Officer (CEO), executive management team and management board. An outline is provided in Appendix A.

In accordance with the standard content for a Risk Management Strategy, the strategic Risk Management Strategy should:

- Define the nature of the organisation and inherent strategic risks that exist
- Specify roles (and, if possible, individuals) that are responsible for strategic risks
- Establish rules for escalating risks from other perspectives to the strategic perspective
- Establish rules for delegating risks from the strategic perspective to other perspectives
- Be appropriate for the size and nature of the organisation, its business and its operating environment
- Ensure that the culture/infrastructure to identify, assess and control risk are put in place

- Set up the mechanism for monitoring the success of the application of the Risk Management Policy (including reports to management, at least annually)
- Ensure that internal control mechanisms are in place for independent assessment that all aspects of the strategy are implemented (and assured).

6.2.5 Reporting

Regular strategic risk reports should be provided to the Accounting Officer/CEO and executive management team. Additional risk reports may be generated when making key business decisions and at the start of business planning cycles.

Strategic risks that exceed tolerances set by the Accounting Officer/CEO are very serious as they will have a significant impact on the proper functioning of the organisation and may even affect its survival. These risks require prompt reporting to the Accounting Officer/CEO. Strategic risks should be escalated to the management board when they exceed the risk tolerance set for the organisation within the strategic Risk Management Strategy.

The strategic perspective must facilitate the escalation of programme, project and operational risks when risk levels exceed agreed tolerances and are, in effect, deemed to affect strategic objectives. It must also facilitate the delegation of strategic risks to programmes, projects and operational areas when risk levels decline and individual risks are no longer deemed strategic.

The strategic perspective should make risk reports available to stakeholders on a regular basis, e.g. annual reports, prospectuses, reports to regulators, parliamentary committees, etc.

6.2.6 Roles and responsibilities

Table 6.2 summarises the roles and responsibilities of those who might be involved in risk management from a strategic perspective. The exact name for each role may vary. The level of resource applied to each role will vary according to the size of the organisation.

Table 6.2 Strategic roles and responsibilities

Role	Responsibilities
Management board	<ul><li>Owns the organisation's Risk Management Policy</li><li>Defines the overall risk appetite for the organisation</li><li>Assures adherence to Risk Management Policy, e.g. reviews statement(s) of internal control (SIC)</li><li>Reviews the strategic Risk Management Strategy</li><li>Approves funding to accommodate strategic risk management</li><li>Monitors the overall organisation risk profile</li><li>Assures clarity of the Accounting Officer/CEO's management of risk accountabilities</li><li>Assists with assessing the risk context for the organisation</li><li>Monitors and acts on escalated strategic risks under the direction of the Accounting Officer/CEO</li><li>Establishes the audit committee as a sub-committee of the board, with a non-executive chair who is also a member of the main board</li><li>Establishes the risk committee as a sub-committee of the board</li></ul>
Accounting Officer (public sector) or CEO (public/private sector)	<ul><li>Ensures that appropriate corporate governance structures and internal control processes are in place</li><li>Ensures that a strategic Risk Management Strategy exists</li><li>Defines and monitors strategic risk tolerances</li><li>Is responsible for the overall implementation of the organisation's Risk Management Policy</li><li>Monitors and assesses the balance within the set of strategic risks</li><li>Owns and manages risks escalated up from the executive management team with the support of the management board</li><li>Ensures that adequate resources are available to implement the strategic Risk Management Strategy</li><li>Agrees what information will be included in the annual accounts specific to the overall management of risk</li><li>Approves the SIC in the annual accounts</li></ul>

	■ Assists the executive management team in embedding the necessary risk management practices
	■ Identifies key risk areas of the organisation and assures that Risk Registers are in place for each
Executive management team	■ Ensures that Risk Registers, a risk review process and an escalation process are in place for designated parts of the organisation
	■ Validates risk assessments
	■ Identifies the need for corporate investment to fund strategic risks
	■ Owns individual strategic risks (as delegated by the Accounting Officer)
	■ Ensures participation in the delivery of risk management within the organisation
	■ Explicitly identifies risk management duties within the terms of engagement of programme, project and operational managers
	■ Agrees with risk specialists the timing, number and content of the risk management interventions
	■ Agrees the timing and content of Risk Progress Reports
	■ Agrees the involvement of the risk manager, audit committee and risk committee as appropriate
	■ Establishes how risk management will be integrated with change control and corporate performance management
Head of the audit committee	■ Defines the Risk Management Policy
	■ Assures management that risk accountabilities exist
	■ Assures compliance with corporate/departmental guidance on internal control
	■ Reviews progress and plans in developing and applying the Risk Management Policy
	■ Reviews the results of the assessments of management of risk that may be part of the process of agreeing the annual SIC
Head of the risk committee	■ Establishes the purpose, terms of reference, committee members, agenda, frequency of meeting and reporting protocols of the risk committee
	■ Chairs the meetings. Agrees what level of risk information will be communicated to the board and how strategic risk information will be escalated to the board between meetings, when circumstances dictate
Risk manager/risk director (alternatively risk facilitator or risk coordinator)	■ Ensures the Risk Management Policy is implemented
	■ Carries out ongoing management of risk maturity assessments
	■ Develops plans to improve the management of risk
	■ Develops management of risk guidance and training
	■ Identifies lessons learned and disseminates learning
	■ Undertakes risk management training and holds seminars to embed risk management
Programme, project and operational boards and senior responsible owners	■ Participate (as appropriate) in the identification, assessment, planning and management of strategic threats and opportunities
	■ Understand the Risk Management Policy and their accountabilities
	■ Implement the Risk Management Policy within their areas of responsibility
	■ Escalate programme, project and operational risks to the strategic perspective as defined by the Risk Management Policy
Risk specialists	■ Prepare strategic Risk Management Strategies
	■ Prepare stakeholder analysis
	■ Prepare a risk breakdown structure or similar
	■ Participate in option analysis
	■ Carry out risk management interventions
	■ Prepare meeting/workshop aids
	■ Facilitate risk meetings/workshops
	■ Identify strategic risks
	■ Undertake qualitative and quantitative assessment of strategic risks
	■ Prepare risk management reports

Internal audit department	■ Makes formal assessments of management of risk implementation (e.g. using the healthcheck at Appendix C or Treasury's Risk Management Assessment Framework) in areas of concern
Staff across the organisation	■ Become aware of the Risk Management Policy ■ Understand their responsibilities in managing risk ■ Participate (as appropriate) in the identification, assessment and control of identified strategic threats and opportunities

6.2.7 Support structure

A central risk function formally responsible for supporting strategic risk management should be identified. In some organisations, this group might be called the corporate planning group, corporate secretariat, portfolio office, or centre of excellence although many other options are possible.

This group supports the Accounting Officer/CEO and executive management team by taking on responsibilities such as:

■ Establishing and maintaining the strategic Risk Management Strategy and strategic Risk Register

■ Helping to balance strategic opportunities and threats relative to the cost implications

■ Supporting the embedding of risk management

■ Providing assurance on different aspects

■ Facilitating risk identification workshops

■ Undertaking some of the techniques that require specialist skills or tools

■ Other (see central risk function in the Risk Management Policy in Chapter 3).

Risk management within the strategic perspective should be supported by processes and teams engaged in:

■ Corporate governance

■ Internal and external audit

■ The secretariat of the management board

■ Corporate risk management (e.g. risk management committee of the management board).

6.2.8 Early warning indicators

The strategic perspective monitors and reports early warning indicators of strategic risk. The early warning indicators will be selected for their relevance to the strategy under scrutiny. Key early warning indicators relate directly to corporate objectives and might include:

■ Finance-related: such as turnover, profitability, operating costs, liquidity and capital expenditure

■ Customer-related: such market share, customer satisfaction and bid loss

■ Growth-related: such as new product development and project failure or success

■ Employee-related: such as turnover and satisfaction

■ Supplier related: such as contract penalties and insurance premium increases

■ Third-party-related: such as insurance premiums, legal action, media coverage and regulator penalties.

Other early warning indicators can be found in change in the organisation's context (e.g. political, economic, social, technological, legal and environmental). Organisations employ tools such as horizon scanning and scenario planning to help monitor the early warning indicators in these areas that are most relevant to the business. These are systematic approaches that bring a range of experts (e.g. subject experts, strategists, futurists, external partners and professionals) together to 'stress test' strategic and business plans. Horizon scanning takes a broader and longer-term view of the context of the organisation to identify strategic risks. The value of the process increases over time as it is repeated, trends evolve, outputs are shared broadly across the organisation, more staff are engaged, methodologies are refined, and horizon scanning skills improve.

6.2.9 Review cycle

The strategic risk management process should be coupled with the business management process. Significant strategic risks should be captured in the organisational or sub-unit business plans.

When making a new corporate investment decision or beginning a new corporate planning cycle, the full risk management process should be applied. A key output from earlier steps will be the strategic Risk Management Strategy, which will define how the management of risk will be handled as part of the current strategic planning cycle or investment decision. As risks are identified and assessed, information will be captured in the strategic Risk Register together with the planned risk responses once these are agreed.

At the end of each business planning cycle, the strategic Risk Management Plan and its implementation should be reviewed for its effectiveness and lessons learned. During subsequent business planning cycles, the risk process should be repeated but lessons learned from earlier iterations should be incorporated.

6.3 PROGRAMME PERSPECTIVE

6.3.1 Organisational context

The programme perspective maintains a view of a significant change to the organisation relative to other changes and relative to the ongoing operations of the organisation.

Programme risks are those risks concerned with transforming business strategy into new ways of working that deliver measurable benefits to the organisation. Stakeholders with an interest in the programme benefits will become aware of the appearance of programme risks.

Programme opportunities and threats are generally identified:

- Through the escalation of risks from projects within the programme
- During programme start-up
- By other programmes with dependencies or interdependencies with this programme
- By operational units affected by the programme.

Programme management typically includes the responsibility for a number of projects. The threat and opportunity trade-offs involved become even more complex as projects compete with one another for resources. The programme management team is primarily responsible for identifying and detailing solutions to conflicts associated with the implementation of strategic plans over which the team has little influence. In addition, the programme management team has to act as 'firefighters' – that is, the team is responsible for keeping specific project crises from getting out of control and affecting the strategic objectives of the organisation.

Typical areas of uncertainty within the programme perspective include:

- Clarity of expected benefits
- The impact of working across organisational boundaries
- Interdependencies between programmes and projects
- Programme funding
- Organisational and cultural issues
- Quality of the benefit-enabling deliverables from projects within the programme
- The impact on business continuity.

6.3.2 Nature of objectives

Programme objectives are principally concerned with achieving desired outcomes in the form of step change improvements to organisational performance. Programme objectives will consist of a mixture of the following types of objectives:

- **Benefits:** these will relate to some form of measurable improvement that is deemed of value by a stakeholder. These objectives may be linked to strategic level key performance indicators where possible. Benefit objectives may be tangible or intangible. Benefit objectives may be expressed in financial or non-financial terms depending on the nature of the benefit.
- **Capability:** these will relate to a business change that develops a new capability, enhances an existing capability, or removes a capability that is no longer desired. Capability objectives will affect the operational performance of the organisation. These objectives should be mapped to projects within the programme that deliver the change.

6.3.3 Stakeholder involvement

Programme stakeholders are likely to include those drawn from the following groups:

- Owners or shareholders, executive management, operational management, and the staff of the organisation who:
  - sponsor the programme
  - have a vested interest in the success of the programme
  - are key beneficiaries
  - supply key enablers to the programme
- Customers or consumers who will be affected by the programme's outcome
- Internal and/or external audit
- Security
- Trade unions
- Political or regulatory bodies
- The wider community in which the affected organisation exists, such as the general public
- Project management teams delivering the projects within the programme
- The programme management team.

Programmes focus on delivering benefits to the organisation and often affect stakeholders from many different internal and external organisational units. Risk management for a programme must be designed to work across appropriate organisational boundaries in order to accommodate and engage stakeholders.

6.3.4 Management of risk approach

Risk management for the programme perspective should be shaped by the Risk Management Policy, programme Risk Management Strategy, and the Risk Management Process Guide.

The Risk Management Strategy for the programme perspective will define how the senior responsible owner, programme director/manager and programme board will handle the management of risk. An outline is provided in Appendix A.

In accordance with the standard content of the Risk Management Strategy, the programme Risk Management Strategy should:

- Identify the owners of the programme and individual projects within the programme
- Identify any additional benefits of adopting risk management within this programme
- Identify the nature and level of risk acceptable within the programme and associated projects
- Clarify rules of escalation from projects to the programme and delegation from programme to projects
- Identify mechanisms for monitoring successful applications of this strategy within the programme and its projects
- Identify how inter-project dependencies will be identified and managed

- Clarify relationships with associated strategies, policies and guidelines.

6.3.5 Reporting

Regular programme risk reports should be provided to the senior responsible owner and programme director/manager. Additional risk reports should be produced at key decision points such as at the end of programme definition and at the end of each tranche of the programme.

Programme risks that exceed tolerances set by the senior responsible owner are serious, as they will have a significant impact on the success of the programme. These risks require prompt reporting to the senior responsible owner and programme board. Programme risks should be escalated to the strategic perspective where they exceed the risk tolerance set for the programme within the programme's Risk Management Strategy.

Project risks should be escalated to the programme against set criteria where they exceed agreed tolerances or where they could affect the achievement of programme objectives.

6.3.6 Roles and responsibilities

Table 6.3 summarises the roles and responsibilities of those who might be involved in risk management from a programme perspective. The exact name for each role may vary. The level of resource applied to each role will vary according to the size of the organisation.

Table 6.3 Programme roles and responsibilities

Role	Responsibilities
Programme board/sponsoring group	■ Ensures adherence within the programme to the organisation's Risk Management Policy ■ Defines the overall risk appetite for the programme investment decision ■ Reviews the programme Risk Management Strategy ■ Approves funding for programme (and associated projects) risk management ■ Monitors the overall programme risk profile ■ Assures clarity of the senior responsible owner's management of risk accountabilities ■ Assists with assessing the risk context for the programme ■ Monitors and acts on risks escalated up by the programme director/programme manager under the direction of the senior responsible owner
Senior responsible owner (SRO)	■ Ensures that risk management structures and processes are in place for the programme ■ Ensures that a designated programme Risk Management Strategy exists ■ Defines and monitors the programme risk tolerances ■ Ensures local implementation of the organisation's Risk Management Policy ■ Monitors and assesses the balance within the set of programme risks ■ Owns and manages risks escalated up from the programme director/manager with the support of the programme board

	■ Agrees when reviews of risk management are required ■ Approves risk management review and assurance reports ■ Assists the programme director/programme manager in embedding the necessary risk management practices ■ Assists with stakeholder management when appropriate to adequately identify stakeholder risks ■ Receives and reviews Risk Progress Reports
Programme director/programme manager	■ Ensures that Risk Registers, a risk review and escalation process are in place for the programme ■ Ensures that adequate management of risk resources are available to implement the programme Risk Management Strategy ■ Validates risk assessments ■ Identifies the need for investment to fund programme risks ■ Owns individual programme risks (as delegated by the senior responsible owner) ■ Ensures the participation in risk management by resources involved with the programme ■ Ensures risk management responsibilities are clearly defined for programme and project team members and are included in job descriptions ■ Agrees with the risk specialists the timing, number, content and techniques of the risk management interventions ■ Agrees the timing and content of Risk Progress Reports ■ Establishes how risk management will be integrated with change control, value management/earned value and performance management
Business change manager	■ Monitors the business-as-usual environment and identifies risks ■ Manages risks associated with maintaining business as usual during the transition period ■ Manages risks associated with the realisation of benefits from the programme outcomes
Programme and project team members	■ Participate (as appropriate) in the identification, assessment, planning and management of identified threats and opportunities ■ Ensure a thorough understanding of individual risk management responsibilities within the team ■ Escalate risks to programme director/manager as defined in the Risk Management Strategy
Business continuity/operations manager/security manager	■ Allocates resources to inform the identification and assessment of risks and the preparation of the programme brief ■ Monitors changes to performance and relevant risks
Assurance teams/Gateway Review Teams	■ Review risk management practices at set intervals as part of a broad programme review or of a specific management of risk review

6.3.7 Support structure

Risk management within a programme may be supported by a programme office. In practice, the office may comprise one or many individuals, depending on the nature of the programme. The programme office supports the programme director/programme manager by taking on some of their responsibilities such as:

■ Establishing and maintaining the programme Risk Management Strategy and the programme Risk Register

■ Helping to balance programme opportunities and threats relative to the benefits

■ Providing assurance of the implementation of the Risk Management Policy.

The programme office may also be able to provide support to the business change manager and the programme/projects teams within the programme by, for example, facilitating risk identification workshops and undertaking some of the techniques that require specialist skills or tools.

6.3.8 Early warning indicators

The programme perspective monitors and reports early warning indicators of programme risk. The early warning indicators will be selected for their relevance to the programme. Key early warning indicators relate directly to programme objectives and might include:

- Achievement of key programme milestones
- Establishment of new capabilities on time and on budget
- Delivery of planned benefits on time and on budget.

Other early warning indicators are changes in the programme's context (e.g. management structures, stakeholders and interdependencies with other programmes).

6.3.9 Review cycle

For a new programme, the risk management process should commence at the outset with key risks captured as part of the programme brief. During programme definition, the full process should be applied with a key output being a programme Risk Management Strategy that defines how the management of risk will be handled during the lifetime of the programme. As risks are identified and assessed, this information will be captured in the programme Risk Register together with the planned risk responses once these are agreed.

At the end of each tranche, the programme Risk Management Strategy should be reviewed for its effectiveness, lessons learned should be documented, and the full risk process should be repeated incorporating lessons learned from earlier iterations.

6.4 PROJECT PERSPECTIVE

6.4.1 Organisational context

The project perspective maintains a view of successfully delivering a predefined output or product and, as a consequence, enabling the delivery of business benefits to the organisation.

Project risks are those risks concerned with delivering defined outputs to an appropriate level of quality within agreed time, cost and scope constraints. The recipients of project outputs will identify the appearance of project risks that will affect the time, cost, quality or scope of outputs.

Project opportunities and threats are generally identified:

- Through the escalation of risks identified when delivering work packages
- During project initiation
- By other projects within a common programme or other projects within the organisation
- By the project's customers and suppliers.

The project perspective is concerned with understanding and defining an approach to address the threats to and maximising the opportunities arising from the objectives established for individual projects. Project risk management is the flexible application of a systematic process to improve the likelihood of a project achieving the pre-agreed objectives. The importance of the project perspective is borne out by successive NAO and OGC reports that describe poor project performance, which, in many cases, is attributable to inadequate or absent management of risk. Projects that exceed their budgets in the private sector can undermine financial performance and in some instances have brought about company collapse.

Typical areas of uncertainty within the project perspective include:

- Availability of skills and key resources
- Clarity of customer requirements and deliverables
- Strength of control and change management processes
- Procurement and acquisition
- The impact on organisational security and safety
- The quality of the project infrastructure
- Scheduling of deliverables.

6.4.2 Nature of objectives

The objectives of project risk management are to inform decision-making during project selection and definition and to improve project performance during design and delivery so that completed projects lead to enhanced organisational performance. The objectives tend to include:

- Time (e.g. delivery by a specified date)
- Cost (e.g. delivery on budget or delivery without penalties from contractors)
- Quality
- Scope.

6.4.3 Stakeholder involvement

Project stakeholders are likely to include those drawn from the following groups:

- Internal and external suppliers
- Customers or recipients of project deliverables
- Political or regulatory bodies
- Project sponsors
- Management
- Team members.

With larger projects (particularly public projects) there may be more than one sponsor (and frequently multiple sponsors) and a number of approval bodies, all of whom will have requirements that need to be understood, captured and integrated (as appropriate) into the project. Complex stakeholder communities such as these introduce risk to a project and need to be explicitly managed.

6.4.4 Management of risk approach

The management of risk for the project perspective should be shaped by the Risk Management Policy, project Risk Management Strategy, and the Risk Management Process Guide. It may also be influenced by the programme Risk Management Strategy where the project forms part of a programme.

The Risk Management Strategy for the project perspective will define how the management of risk will be handled during the lifetime of the project. An outline is provided in Appendix A.

In addition to the standard content of the Risk Management Strategy, the project Risk Management Strategy should:

■ Reference the programme Risk Management Strategy (if applicable)

■ Identify any additional benefits associated with the adoption of management of risk for this project

■ Identify relationships with associated programmes, projects, policies and standards

■ Identify any contractual relationships with third parties and how the associated risks need to be managed.

6.4.5 Reporting

Regular project risk reports should be provided to the senior responsible owner and project manager. Additional

risk reports should be produced at key decision points such as at project initiation and after completion of stages.

Throughout the life of a project the sponsor (or sponsors) will require updates on the progress being made. Typically they will seek a detailed progress report at key stages throughout the project lifecycle, to enable them to decide if they wish to continue, suspend or terminate the project.

Risk management is a key tool in the decision-making process at these key stages, as it will inform the sponsor(s) of (for instance):

■ The risk exposure of alternative options under consideration

■ The size of the contingency that needs to be set aside for risk events

■ The most serious risks facing the project at any one time

■ The primary sources of risk

■ The likelihood of success against the schedule and budget (this is accomplished by the preparation of quantitative analysis including simulation and the calculation of percentiles)

■ The risk response actions required to address the identified risks

■ The need to increase funding of the project

■ Where management time will generate the greatest benefits for the project.

6.4.6 Roles and responsibilities

Table 6.4 summarises the roles and responsibilities of those who might be involved in risk management from a project perspective. The exact name for each role may vary. The level of resource applied to each role will vary according to the size of the organisation.

Table 6.4 Project roles and responsibilities

Role	Responsibilities
Project board	■ Ensures adherence within the project to the organisation's Risk Management Policy ■ Defines the overall risk appetite for the project investment decision ■ Reviews the project Risk Management Strategy ■ Approves funding for project (and associated stage) risk management ■ Monitors the overall project risk profile ■ Assures clarity of the senior responsible owner's management of risk accountabilities ■ Assists with assessing the risk context for the project ■ Monitors and acts on risks escalated up by the project manager under the direction of the senior responsible owner
Senior responsible owner (SRO) (sometimes known as project sponsor)	■ Ensures that risk management structures and processes are in place for the project ■ Ensures that a project Risk Management Strategy exists ■ Defines and monitors the project risk tolerances

	■ Ensures local implementation of the organisation's Risk Management Policy
	■ Monitors and assesses the balance within the set of project risks
	■ Owns and manages risks escalated up from project team members
	■ Agrees when reviews of risk management are required
	■ Approves risk management review and assurance reports
	■ Assists the project manager in embedding the necessary risk management practices
	■ Assists with stakeholder management when appropriate to adequately identify stakeholder risks
	■ Receives and reviews Risk Progress Reports
Project manager	■ Ensures that Risk Registers, a risk review, and escalation processes are in place for each programme _project_
	■ Ensures that adequate management of risk resources are available to implement the project Risk Management Strategy
	■ Validates risk assessments
	■ Identifies the need for investment to fund project risks
	■ Owns individual project risks (as delegated by the senior responsible owner)
	■ Ensures participation in risk management by the resources involved with the project
	■ Explicitly identifies risk management duties within the terms of engagement of programme and project team members
	■ Agrees with the risk specialists the timing, number and content of the risk management interventions
	■ Agrees the timing and content of Risk Progress Reports
	■ Agrees the involvement of the risk specialists, e.g. feasibility study, assessment of options, calculation of contingencies, selection of the procurement route, evaluation of the risk ownership profile of different contracts, preparation of tender documents and reviewing returned tenders
	■ Establishes how risk management will be integrated with change control, value management/earned value and performance management
Project team members	■ Participate (as appropriate) in the identification, assessment, planning and management of identified threats and opportunities
	■ Ensure a thorough understanding of the individual risk management responsibilities within the team
	■ Escalate risks to project manager as defined in the project Risk Management Strategy
Business continuity manager/operations manager/security manager	■ Allocates resources to inform the identification and assessment of risks and the preparation of the project brief
	■ Monitors changes to performance and relevant risks
Assurance teams/Gateway Review Teams	■ Review risk management practices at set intervals as part of a broad project review or of a specific management of risk review

6.4.7 Support structure

Risk management within a project may be supported by a project office. In practice, the office may comprise one or many individuals depending on the nature of the project. The project office supports the project manager by taking on some of their responsibilities such as:

■ Establishing and maintaining the project Risk Management Strategy and the project Risk Register

■ Helping to balance project opportunities and threats relative to the cost implications

■ Providing assurance of the implementation of the Risk Management Policy.

The project office may also be able to provide support to the business change manager and the programme/projects teams within the programme by, for example, facilitating risk identification workshops and undertaking some of the techniques that require specialist skills or tools.

For project risk management to be effective, it needs the full support of the project team. The team's most important contribution will be identifying and assessing the risks in terms of their probability and impact, and defining specific response actions to the risks identified. Risk management relies on the collective knowledge and experience of the project team initially to think through the threats that could derail the project and consider which opportunities might be maximised to enhance performance. Subsequently the team will be required to derive responses to the risks, which could be very wide ranging, for example, from changing the procurement route or contract to using different materials or suppliers.

6.4.8 Early warning indicators

The project perspective monitors and reports early warning indicators of project risk. The early warning indicators will be selected for their relevance to the project, will relate to critical aspects of the project, and take account of the duration of the project. Key early warning indicators relate directly to the project's objectives and might include a combination of the following:

- Design packages accomplished to schedule/late
- Approvals accomplished to schedule/late
- Subcontract packages let to schedule/late
- Major supplier performance
- Major subcontractor performance
- Contractor performance
- Adherence to budget (e.g. rate of spend behind or ahead of planned spend)
- Spend against degree of completion
- Adherence to schedule (e.g. days ahead or behind schedule)
- Milestones accomplished to schedule/missed
- Staff turnover
- Claims submitted
- Stoppages
- Increases in staff skills, motivation, morale or loyalty.

The objective of early warning indicators on a project is to provide information to enable corrective or mitigation actions to take place. The indicators must be updated on a regular cycle and any action thought appropriate must be implemented swiftly to ensure it will have an impact. Project participants must be advised at the outset of the project what the indicators are and what information is to be collected to be conveyed against the indicator, the reporting frequency, and that corrective action will be required when necessary to implement project changes to achieve the project objectives.

6.4.9 Review cycle

For a new project, the risk management process should commence at the outset with key risks captured as part of the start-up process. During project initiation, the full process should be applied and a key output will be a project Risk Management Strategy that defines how the management of risk will be handled during the lifetime of the project. As risks are identified and assessed, this information will be captured in the project Risk Register together with the planned risk responses once these are agreed.

The project Risk Management Strategy will record the timing of the risk management interventions to be undertaken during and at the end of each of the project stages (e.g. gateway reviews prior to the commencement of the next project stage). The project Risk Management Strategy will record the activities to be completed during each intervention and specifically the risk process steps to be undertaken. It is not uncommon for interventions late in the project lifecycle to update (and repeat) risk process steps carried out during earlier interventions, to reflect the improved level of information available. Early risk interventions will focus on the assessment of alternative proposals. Subsequent interventions will assess alternative procurement routes and their inherent risk profiles and confidence levels in achieving the objectives. Successive interventions will also be used to define appropriate responses. Each subsequent intervention will show whether the level of risk exposure of the project is improving or deteriorating by the monitoring of trends.

The depth of risk management to be applied at each of the interventions will be dictated by:

- The importance of the project to the client (in terms of possible impact on the bottom line, reputation, media attention, shareholder expectations, market confidence, partnership relationships, share value or other project dependencies)
- The potential losses or the implications of not having completed the project by a particular date
- The project value, degree of complexity or physical size
- The rate of change occurring in the context of the project (e.g. marketplace)
- The degree of novel technology included in the project.

At the end of each stage, the project Risk Management Strategy should be reviewed for its effectiveness, lessons learned should be documented, and the full risk process should be repeated incorporating lessons learned from earlier iterations.

6.5 OPERATIONAL PERSPECTIVE

6.5.1 Organisational context

The operational perspective maintains a view of the people, processes, and technologies that support ongoing business-as-usual or service delivery activities of the organisation in relation to customer expectations. In this context, services may be delivered to internal customers (e.g. by a human resources function) or to external customers (e.g. financial management services by a money management firm). The operational perspective also monitors how strategic changes to the organisation affect ongoing business-as-usual and service delivery activities.

Operational risks are those concerned with maintaining an appropriate level of business service to existing and new customers. Customers receiving the affected business service will recognise the appearance of operational risks.

Operational opportunities and threats are generally identified:

- Through the escalation of risks from business or service delivery teams (e.g. engineering, information systems, finance, human resources, security, fraud, customer support, etc.)
- By service-enabling suppliers
- By service-receiving customers.

Operational risks relate to all internal and external services, and will vary from organisation to organisation. A number of factors contribute to the operational risk profile within an organisation, including the use (or lack) of a standardised approach, management endorsement, employee awareness and education, the attitude to risk within the organisation, risk appetite and the culture of the organisation.

In order to protect organisations from operational risks, a framework of operational controls should be established. These controls ensure that the operational aspects of the organisation are conducted in an appropriate manner and the correct checks and balances are in place. These operational controls are subject to a number of threats (for example, failure to adhere to policy or follow procedures, lack of segregation of duties, and failure to monitor events), but the controls are put in place to protect the organisation from operational risks. Examples of controls may include multiple signatures for cheques, different authorisation levels for expenditure, credit/trade vetting of suppliers and customers, and adherence to specific standards.

Risk management needs to become ingrained within the day-to-day operational activities of any organisation and in order to be successful, it requires monitoring, measurement, control, people who understand and process risks, and discipline.

The objectives of the operational perspective of risk management are to identify and manage the risks within the management of the organisation, and ensure the selection and implementation of suitable risk response options that will address the risks within an organisation in an appropriate way. The operational perspective of risk management should also aim to identify any potential threats to the management of the organisation, along with the potential opportunities to improve the operations of the organisation and achieve its business objectives more efficiently or quickly.

Typical areas of uncertainty within the operational perspective include:

- The strength of operational controls for cost and quality
- Clarity of service requirements and definition
- The quality of the infrastructure to provide the required operational services
- The skills and availability of human resources to support the required service provision
- The strength of contracts and contract management processes that support the required level of service provision
- Changes to service requirements and the ability to manage in a controlled way
- The quality of new product development (i.e. quality of consideration of service implementation, handover, maintenance and decommissioning)
- Expectations of service users
- Incident handling mechanisms
- Business continuity or contingency measures with regard to maintaining (critical) business services
- Investment in infrastructure to support future needs/opportunities
- Legal or contractual obligations.

6.5.2 Nature of objectives

Operational objectives are concerned with the successful day-to-day management of the organisation. Objectives generally relate to specific levels of service delivery performance and improvements to organisational performance. Operational objectives may therefore consider:

- Reputation
- Volume (e.g. customers or units produced)
- Cost (e.g. per unit produced)

- Quality (e.g. unit or process failures)
- Internal control (e.g. health, safety or failure)
- Revenue
- Staff (e.g. satisfaction)
- Customer (e.g. churn, satisfaction).

6.5.3 Stakeholder involvement

Operational stakeholders are likely to include those drawn from the following groups:

- Owners or shareholders, executive management, operational management, and staff of the organisation who are responsible for:
  - the delivery of products/services
  - activities supporting the delivery of products/services
  - implementing, maintaining and monitoring internal controls
  - supplying goods or services to the department or organisation
- Customers or consumers who will be affected by the services/products delivered
- Counterparties
- Business partners and suppliers
- Other departments, divisions or offices
- Internal and/or external audit
- Compliance departments
- Security
- Health and safety
- Business continuity
- Trade unions
- Political or regulatory bodies
- The wider community in which the affected organisation exists, such as the general public
- Project and programme management teams delivering projects and programmes.

6.5.4 Management of risk approach

Risk management for the operational perspective should be shaped by the Risk Management Policy, operational Risk Management Strategy and Risk Management Process Guide.

The Risk Management Strategy for the operational perspective will define how risk management will be handled during the lifetime of the operational unit or service. An outline is provided in Appendix A. In particular, it is used to show close links to security, health and safety, business continuity and contingency plans.

In accordance with the standard content of the Risk Management Strategy, the operational Risk Management Strategy should:

- Define the risk owner for individual services encompassed by this strategy
- Identify any additional benefits associated with adopting management of risk for the operations/services covered
- Confirm the scope of the strategy (e.g applied to a single service or a range of operational services)
- Identify the types of service risk to be managed
- Clarify roles and responsibilities for managing operational risk, in particular, security, health and safety, and business continuity
- Ensure that operational contingencies are covered as part of the support to overall risk management
- Make cross-references to the details of the operations covered.

6.5.5 Reporting

Operational risk reporting is fundamental to an organisation's understanding of its exposure to risks and how it is managing them. Operational management and independent personnel, such as internal/external audit, should conduct regular reviews against operational controls to ensure these controls are appropriate, complete and are being adhered to.

Every member of staff within the organisation should be responsible for reporting a breach in an internal control and identifying additional risks. These should be swiftly recorded and escalated to management for assessment, control and, if they exceed the risk tolerance levels, further escalation or notification to senior management. The management team should provide exception reports against the controls on a regular basis and identify any additional risks and how they have been assessed and treated.

6.5.6 Roles and responsibilities

Table 6.5 summarises the roles and responsibilities of those who might be involved in risk management from an operational perspective. The exact name for each role may vary. The level of resource applied to each role will vary according to the size of the organisation.

Table 6.5 Operational roles and responsibilities

Role	Responsibilities
Executive management team	■ Ensures that key operational/service areas are adhering to the organisation's Risk Management Policy ■ Defines the overall risk appetite for operational areas ■ Reviews key operational Risk Management Strategies, as appropriate ■ Approves funding for operational risk management (and specific operational risk functions such as business continuity management) ■ Monitors the overall operational risk profile ■ Assures clarity of the operational director/head of operations' management of risk accountabilities ■ Assists with the assessment of the risk context for the operational area ■ Monitors and acts on risks escalated up by the operational managers under the direction of the operational director/head of operations
Operational director/head of operations (or head of other specific operational function)	■ Ensures risk management structures and appropriate internal control procedures are in place for key operational/service areas ■ Ensures that designated operational Risk Management Strategies exist ■ Defines and monitors operational risk tolerances ■ Ensures local implementation of the organisation's Risk Management Strategies ■ Monitors and assesses the balance within the set of operational risks ■ Owns and manages risks escalated up from operational managers with the support of the executive management team ■ Agrees when reviews of risk management are required ■ Approves risk management review and assurance reports ■ Assists operational managers in embedding the necessary risk management practices ■ Assists with stakeholder management, when appropriate, to adequately expose stakeholder risks ■ Receives and reviews Risk Progress Reports
Operational managers (e.g. business facilities manager, human resource manager, legal and regulatory officer, information security manager, software engineering, or procurement manager)	■ Assure that Risk Registers, a risk review, and an escalation process are in place for designated parts of the organisation ■ Ensure that adequate management of risk resources are available to implement the operational Risk Management Strategy ■ Validate risk assessments ■ Identify the need for investments to fund operational risks ■ Own the individual operational risks (as delegated by operational director/head of operations) ■ Ensure participation in risk management by the resources involved with specific operational or service areas ■ Ensure risk management responsibilities are clearly defined for operations or service delivery staff and are included in job descriptions ■ Agree with the risk specialists the timing, number and content of risk management interventions ■ Agree the timing and content of Risk Progress Reports ■ Agree the involvement of the risk specialists e.g. feasibility studies, assessment of options, calculation of contingencies, selection of the procurement route, evaluation of the risk ownership profile of different contracts, preparation of tender documents, and reviewing returned tenders ■ Establish how risk management will be integrated within the business processes
Assurance team including internal/external audit	■ Reviews risk management practices at set intervals as part of a broad programme review or of a specific management of risk review ■ Reviews operational risk controls ■ Reviews control effectiveness

| Risk specialists (e.g. business continuity manager, crisis manager, security manager, health and safety officer, or finance manager) | ■ Execute duties specified in the Risk Management Policy and operational Risk Management Strategy
■ Maintain designated risk, issues and incidents registers
■ Review and escalate risks as appropriate
■ Contribute to the development of the operational Risk Management Strategies as appropriate
■ Formally allocate specialist resources to support the risk management processes
■ Identify and assess specialist risks
■ Conduct specialist risk assessments and risk reports
■ Assure organisational adherence to legislation and report deficiencies to the risk manager/director (see strategic perspective for description of this role)
■ Identify appropriate legislation requirements
■ Assess the effectiveness of risk analysis and management, and provide recommendations for improvement |
| Operations team members | ■ Participate (as appropriate) in the identification, assessment and control of identified operational threats and opportunities |

6.5.7 Support structure

Risk management within an operational area may be supported by a business office. In practice, the office may comprise one or many individuals depending on the nature of the operational unit. The business office supports the operational director/head of operations by taking on some of their responsibilities such as:

■ Establishing and maintaining the operational Risk Management Strategy and the operational Risk Register

■ Helping to balance project opportunities and threats relative to the cost implications

■ Providing assurance of the implementation of the Risk Management Policy.

The business office may also be able to provide support to operations managers and the operations teams members within the operational area by, for example, facilitating risk identification workshops and undertaking some of the techniques that require specialist skills or tools. This office may also be able to provide support, education and awareness to the operational staff.

Correct and timely actions towards risks are essential for an organisation to minimise the negative and maximise the positive influences of risk. An essential element in achieving this is the necessary escalation and communication of risks through or across the organisation structure. Individual and positional responsibilities for identifying, communicating and addressing risk must be clearly defined and communicated to individuals so that each individual knows whether they can address the risk themselves (or make decisions on addressing the risk), or whether they need to escalate the risk to an other individual (and if so, to whom).

6.5.8 Early warning indicators

The operational perspective monitors early warning indicators of operational risk. The early warning indicators will be selected for their relevance to the service. Key early warning indicators relate directly to operational objectives and might include:

■ Customer churn

■ Staff turnover

■ Levels of overtime of staff

■ Achievement of service quality levels

■ Achievement of unit cost targets

■ Achievement of volume targets

■ Achievement of delivery on time targets

■ Achievement of revenue targets

■ Levels of safety incidents or injury

■ Incidents of plant or process failure.

6.5.9 Review cycle

For a new service, the risk management process should commence at the outset with the key risks captured as part of the concept identification. During subsequent definition, the full process should be applied with a key output being an operational Risk Management Strategy that defines how the management of risk will be handled during the lifetime of the service. As risks are identified and assessed, this information will be captured in the operational Risk Register together with the planned risk responses once they are agreed.

The risk management process should be embedded within operational/service delivery activities of the organisation and should be supported and owned by a member of the executive management team.

At the end of each service review point, the operational Risk Management Strategy should be reviewed for its effectiveness, lessons learned should be documented, and the full risk process should be repeated incorporating lessons learned from earlier iterations.

Management of risk document outlines A

Appendix A: Management of risk document outlines

The following outlines describe the purpose of some of the key management documents that form part of the management of risk framework, together with a summary of the typical contents.

A1 COMMUNICATIONS PLAN

Purpose

To describe how information will be disseminated to, and recovered from, all stakeholders of a particular organisational activity.

Composition

Typically a Communications Plan will include:

- Key elements of information to be distributed
- Roles and responsibilities for communication
- List of stakeholders and information requirements
- Communication mechanisms
- Process for handling feedback
- Schedule of communication activities.

A2 ISSUE LOG

Purpose

To capture and maintain information in a consistent, structured manner on all of the identified issues that have already occurred and require action. These issues may include risks that have materialised and have changed from possible events to actual events.

Composition

Typically an Issue Log will include as a minimum:

- Issue identifier
- Issue category
- Issue description
- Impact
- Action required
- Date action to be implemented
- Date action implemented
- Issue owner
- Issue actionee.

For more information see Chapter 3, Management of Risk Approach.

A3 RISK IMPROVEMENT PLAN

Purpose

To provide a record of the current status of management of risk cultural awareness within the organisation, the behavioural targets that are to be achieved and an appropriate time period in which to achieve them, and the mechanisms/methods planned to be used to achieve the cultural change (these need to be appropriate to the culture and ethos of the organisation).

Composition

Typically a Risk Improvement Plan will include as a minimum:

- Current date
  (The date the cultural plan is agreed or the date the existing behaviour is assessed and recorded.)
- Category group
  (The group of individuals being targeted for this particular improvement initiative, e.g. executives, senior managers, technical staff or secretaries.)
- Existing behaviours
  (A description detailing the assessment of current behaviour towards the different aspects of management of risk.)
- Target behaviour
  (A description detailing the preferred/target behaviour towards the different aspects of management of risk.)
- Target date
  (The time by which you wish to target the change in behaviour.)
- Mechanisms
  (The mechanisms that will be used to change the behaviour towards or understanding of management of risk.)
- Measurement
  (How the change in behaviour will be measured.)

A4   RISK MANAGEMENT STRATEGY

Purpose

The purpose of a Risk Management Strategy is to describe for a particular organisational activity the specific risk management activities that will be undertaken.

Composition

Typically a strategy document will include:

- Introduction
- Outline of the activity
- Roles and responsibilities
- The process
- Scales for estimating probability and impact
- Probability
- Impact
- Expected value
- Proximity
- Risk response category
- Budget required
- Tools and techniques
- Templates
- Early warning indicators
- Timing of risk management activities
- Reporting
- Glossary of terms
- Checklists and prompt lists.

For more information see Chapter 3, Management of Risk Approach.

A5   RISK MANAGEMENT POLICY

Purpose

To communicate how risk management will be implemented throughout an organisation (or part of an organisation) to support the realisation of its strategic objectives.

Composition

Typically a policy will include:

- Introduction
- Risk appetite and capacity
- Risk tolerance thresholds
- Procedure for escalation
- Roles and responsibilities
- Glossary of terms
- Risk management process

- Early warning indicators
- Tools and techniques to support the process
- When risk management should be implemented
- Reporting
- Budget
- Quality assurance
- Annual review
- Additional information sources.

For more information see Chapter 3, Management of Risk Approach.

A6   RISK MANAGEMENT PROCESS GUIDE

Purpose

To describe the series of steps (from Identify through to Implement) and their respective associated activities necessary to implement risk management.

Composition

Typically a process document will include as a minimum:

- Introduction
- Roles and responsibilities
- Steps in the process
- Tools and techniques
- Templates
- Glossary of terms.

It may also include:

- Early warning indicators
- How contingencies will be defined
- Owners of contingencies.

For more information see Chapter 3, Management of Risk Approach.

A7   RISK PROGRESS REPORT

Purpose

To provide regular progress information to management on risk management within a particular activity.

Composition

Typically a progress report will include as a minimum:

- Progress of planned risk management actions
- Effectiveness of implemented actions
- Trend analysis of closed and new risks
- Insurance requirements

- Spend against contingencies
- Spend against response action budgets
- Numbers of risks emerging in the different risk categories
- Movement of risk against the key performance indicators
- Anticipated emerging risks that will require specific management attention.

This information may be incorporated within other progress reports if appropriate.

A8 RISK REGISTER

Purpose

To capture and maintain information on all of the identified threats and opportunities relating to a specific organisational activity.

Composition

Typically a Risk Register will include:

- Risk identifier
- Risk category
- Risk cause
- Risk event (threat or opportunity)
- Risk effect (description in words of the impact)
- Probability (pre-response action)
- Probability (post-response action)
- Impact (pre-response action)
- Impact (post-response action)
- Expected value (pre-response action)
- Expected value (post-response action)
- Proximity
- Risk response categories
- Risk response actions
- Residual risk
- Risk status
- Risk owner
- Risk actionee.

For more information see Chapter 3, Management of Risk Approach.

A9 RISK RESPONSE PLAN

Purpose

To record details of all risk response actions and to help with the monitoring and control of these actions. This is an optional document as it may be decided to hold this information with the Risk Register against each risk.

Composition

Typically a response plan will include as a minimum:

- Risk ID
- Risk description
- Impact in terms of cost and time
- Response category
- Actions to respond to the threat or opportunity (it is common for there to be multiple actions)
- Risk owner
- Risk actionee
- Date by which the actions are to be implemented
- Anticipated cost of the response
- Any secondary threats or opportunities that it is anticipated may arise from the response.

A10 STAKEHOLDER MAP

Purpose

To document all parties (individuals or groups) who have an interest in the outcome of the proposed activity. This may include individuals or groups outside the business. The interests of each stakeholder are identified and the map is used to ensure all interests are catered for, which includes keeping them informed and accepting feedback.

The Stakeholder Map is output from the culmination of work undertaken on stakeholder analysis. A stakeholder is anyone affected by a decision and interested in its outcome. This can include individuals or groups, both inside and outside the organisation. The stakeholder analysis is a piece of work undertaken to assess the influence and importance of each individual stakeholder or stakeholder group. The Stakeholder Map is typically shown as a matrix, detailing individual stakeholders or groups of stakeholders and their particular interests, along with the communication route and frequency for each stakeholder or group of stakeholders.

Composition

Typically a Stakeholder Map will include as a minimum:

- List of stakeholders
- List of interests (i.e. the issues that concern them, their attitude towards aspects of the situation that present a risk, and the extent to which they can influence the way that the risk is addressed)
- Matrix of stakeholders to interest and the relative importance of the project/magnitude of the risks to each.

Common techniques B

Appendix B: Common techniques

B1 INTRODUCTION

This appendix provides an overview of the wide choice of techniques that are available to assist in undertaking the management of risk process.

These techniques may be supported by one or more tools. The distinction made between techniques and tools is that techniques are implementation aids to carry out steps in the management of risk process whereas tools are commercial off-the-shelf software products that carry out routines and statistical analysis at high speed to support techniques.

Collectively these tools and techniques have a series of benefits enabling those engaging in risk management to capture information in a consistent way, provide more thorough and reliable results, accelerate the process, articulate options, prioritise actions, improve communication and produce an audit trail. The tools and techniques are not an end in themselves, but can be powerful aids to support the management of risk.

B2 SELECTION OF TECHNIQUES

The selection of techniques is loosely analogous to selecting a tool from a tool bag. You don't need all of the tools at the same time and each tool is suitable for a specific task. There is now a considerable range of techniques to choose from. Sometimes choosing the most appropriate technique is obvious (e.g. when to use net present value), but sometimes the choice is not straightforward (for example, when would you choose brainstorming, or the Nominal Group Technique, or the Delphi Technique?).

The choice of technique should be based on:

■ The purpose or goal of undertaking the risk management activity. For instance, is the goal of the risk management study to select between options, calculate a contingency or to establish the likelihood of an activity being completed on time?
■ The size or stage of the activity being undertaken.
■ The familiarity of the user with the technique's application, the amount of time available for the risk study, the level of detail that the sponsor requires and the use to which the risk management outputs will be put.

■ The familiarity of the participants with the risk management process, the degree to which risk management is embedded in the organisation and the willingness of the participants to support the technique.
■ The availability of information or data to be able to use the techniques in a meaningful way.
■ The ability of the user of the technique to explain its method of application and the results to the sponsor. A lack of confidence in the results will render them worthless.
■ Its cost, ease of use, availability and applicability.

Similarly the selection of risk software tools requires careful consideration. Appendix F provides a suggested approach for selecting tools.

B3 TECHNIQUES FOR THE IDENTIFY – CONTEXT STEP

The Context step is concerned with understanding the context of the organisational activity under examination and the techniques used for this step are all about improving our understanding of the background to the activity's initiation, its objectives, scope, lifecycle, funding, the participants, the constraints and the approvals required.

Project lifecycle

For the project perspective, project lifecycles can be an invaluable tool in mapping the activities within a project and the subsequent identification of the sources of risk associated with each activity. Examples of descriptions of project lifecycles are:

■ RIBA plan of work
  ● The Architect's Plan of Work, Roland Phillips, RIBA Publishing, June 2000.

■ OGC Successful Delivery Toolkit™ project lifecycle and the OGC Gateway Project Review Process
  ● The OGC developed the Gateway Project Review Process and introduced it across central civil government as part of the modernisation agenda to support the delivery of improved public services. The process has been operating since January 2001. The Gateway Project Review Process applies to construction/property projects, IT-enabled business change projects, projects that procure services and procurements utilising framework contracts.

The project lifecycle is required to support the construction of risk breakdown structures.

Process map

Process mapping is used to describe in workflow diagrams and supporting text, every vital step in a business process. Only too often an organisation believes it knows its business processes, when in reality managers do not really understand them or the risks that individual processes add to an organisation's overall business exposure. Process mapping was introduced as an analytical and communication tool to understand and improve existing processes and enable organisations to reconfigure their processes to improve performance. Preparing a high-level process map can be a catalyst in terms of stimulating thinking about the sources of risk.

PEST prompt

PEST is an acronym for Political, Economic, Social and Technological factors. This tool can help uncover external risk exposure. Completing a PEST analysis is very simple and can be undertaken during a workshop or as part of a brainstorming session. A PEST analysis measures a market (whereas a SWOT analysis measures a business unit, a proposition or an idea). The PEST model can be expanded to include Legislative and Environmental (or Ecological) factors, which changes the acronym to PESTLE. Adding one more factor, Industry analysis, changes the model to PESTELI. In order for the PEST analysis to be effective, the subject must be clearly defined before the participants commence the analysis, to ensure that they fully understand the goals. The PEST analysis subject should be a clear definition of the market under review and from which standpoint: a company looking at its market; a specific business unit; a product in relation to its market; a brand in relation to its market; a strategic option or an investment opportunity.

SWOT prompt

A SWOT analysis can be used to draw out the threats and opportunities facing an enterprise and has the advantage of being quick to implement and readily understood. Analysis of the strengths, weaknesses, opportunities and threats brings together the results of both internal company analysis and external environmental analysis. Common and beneficial applications of SWOT are gaining a greater understanding and insight into competitors and market position. The results of a PEST analysis (discussed above) can be used to inform the environmental analysis. The process of creating a SWOT analysis is valuable because it involves discussion among the key managers in the business. It stimulates thinking that is not overly structured or restrictive.

The results of the analysis are typically captured on a diagram such as Figure B.1.

Pursuit of opportunities may add to the organisation's strengths and threats may contribute to existing or new weaknesses.

Figure B.1 SWOT analysis

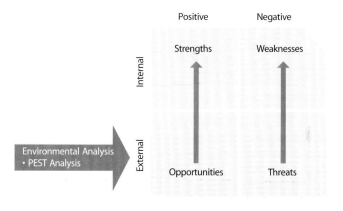

RACI diagram to support stakeholder analysis

A RACI diagram is used to describe the roles and responsibilities of the participants in a business or project activity in terms of producing predetermined deliverables. RACI is an acronym formed from the four participatory roles that it describes:

- **R**esponsible (those who undertake the activity, the resources)
- **A**ccountable (those who take the credit for success or responsibility for failure, the 'activity manager' – there must be at least one **A** specified for each activity)
- **C**onsulted (those whose opinions are sought)
- **I**nformed (those who are kept up-to-date on progress).

A simplified example of a RACI diagram is illustrated in Figure B.2.

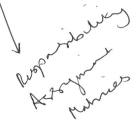

Figure B.2 RACI diagram ~~Names of people~~

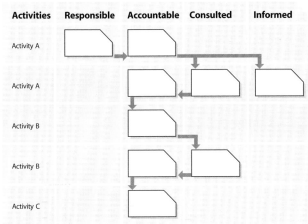

There is an expanded version, RACI-VS, which adds two roles:

- **V**erifies (the party who checks whether the product meets the quality criteria set forth in the product description)
- **S**igns off (the party who approves the **V** decision and authorises the product hand-off).

Stakeholder matrix

Stakeholders are those individuals or groups who will be affected by an activity, programme or project. They could include senior managers whose business areas are directly or indirectly involved, the end-users (including customers outside the organisation), suppliers and partners. Effective management of the stakeholders' interests includes the resolution of conflicting objectives and representation of end-users who may not be directly involved in the activity. Stakeholders' interests can be managed through stakeholder meetings and specific user panels providing input to a requirement specification. The key objective is to capture, align, record, sign-off and deliver stakeholder objectives. A way of prioritising this activity is to use a stakeholder matrix. A possible format for a stakeholder matrix is included in Figure B.3.

Figure B.3 Power impact matrix

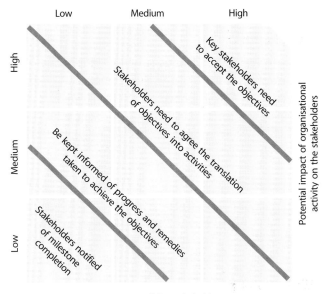

Importance of the stakeholders to the organisational activity

B4 TECHNIQUES FOR THE IDENTIFY – IDENTIFY THE RISKS STEP

The Identify the risks step is concerned with identifying the threats and opportunities relating to the activity under review and the techniques used in this step are all about improving our understanding of the sources of the threats and opportunities specific to this activity. Techniques for this step are aimed at improving our knowledge of threat and opportunity events that occurred on previous similar activities or enhancing our awareness of lessons learned to inform proactive management requirements.

Risk Potential Assessment

The Risk Potential Assessment (available at www.ogc.gov.uk) was developed by the Cabinet Office to identify typical problem areas and criticality to an organisation in terms of the scale of a project against central criteria. In using the technique, you are required to build in your organisation's specific perceptions of risk for the project, such as visibility to the public, in order to assess your organisation's exposure to risk.

Risk checklist

A risk checklist is an in-house list of risks that were identified or occurred during previous organisational activities. Risk checklists are often developed from managers' past experience. They permit managers to capture lessons learned and assess whether similar risks are relevant to the organisation's current activities. Checklists should not be viewed as an exhaustive list of risks as they will not capture the specific circumstances of the activity being examined.

Risk prompt list

A risk prompt list, as described by the first edition of the PRAM Guide (APM 1997), is a list that 'categorises risks into types or areas'. The HM Treasury guide known as the Orange Book provides a schedule of what it considers the most common categories of risk, with examples of source and effect for each category. This revised categorisation of risk is based on the PESTLE model as described at www.strategy.gov.uk. Authors Cooper, Day and Holliwell also suggest risk categories, as does BSI publication PD 6668. As with checklists, prompt lists have to be used with caution, as they do not provide an exhaustive list of categories and have to be expanded to suit the specific context of the activity under examination.

Lessons learned logs and reports

Project participants compile lessons learned logs (typically tables or schedules) during the course of projects to capture informally events as they arise, so they are not forgotten and can be used to inform subsequent projects on what went well and what did not go well and should not be repeated. Lessons learned reports are compiled at the end of projects and describe the lessons learned. Lessons learned reports are far more structured than logs, are based on descriptive narratives and expand on the information contained in the logs. They are signed off by senior management and are held centrally for review prior to the commencement of new projects. They provide a valuable and rich source of risks and mitigation actions.

Risk breakdown structure

A valuable technique used in uncovering the sources of risk is a business risk breakdown structure (BRBS) which may be described as 'a hierarchical decomposition of the business environment through to business processes, assembled to illustrate potential sources of risk. It organises and defines the total extent of organisational or project operations established to accomplish the business objectives. Each descending level represents an increasingly detailed definition of sources of risk to the business.' Business risk breakdown structures have their roots in project management work breakdown structures (WBS).

Risk taxonomy

The business risk taxonomy (BRT) provides a framework for studying business management issues and is a structure for eliciting risks from commonly recognised risk sources in the business environment. The business risk taxonomy provides a structured checklist that organises known enterprise risks into general classes subdivided into elements and attributes. Attributes can be further subdivided into features if this is found to be productive. A taxonomy enables threat and opportunity to be broken down into manageable components that can then be aggregated for exposure measurement, management and reporting purposes. The business risk taxonomy is based on a software risk taxonomy developed by the Software Engineering Institute of Carnegie Mellon University, Pittsburgh, Pennsylvania, US.

Risk identification workshop

A risk identification workshop is a group session designed to focus on a particular organisational activity for the identification of risks. The workshop should be facilitated by an experienced risk practitioner, who should employ particular identification techniques and share the benefit of in-depth programme and project experience. This should lead to a broad range of risks being identified, with a view of possible risk owners emerging.

Cause and effect diagrams

Cause and effect diagrams, also known as fish-bone diagrams, are graphical representations of the causes of various events that lead to one or more impacts. Each diagram may possess several start points (A points) and one or more end points (B points). Construction of the diagram may begin from an A point and work towards a B point or extrapolate backwards from a B point. This is largely a matter of preference. Some people prefer to start with an impact (B point) and work backwards to its cause. Others prefer to start with an event (A point) and work towards an impact.

Figure B.4 Cause and effect diagram

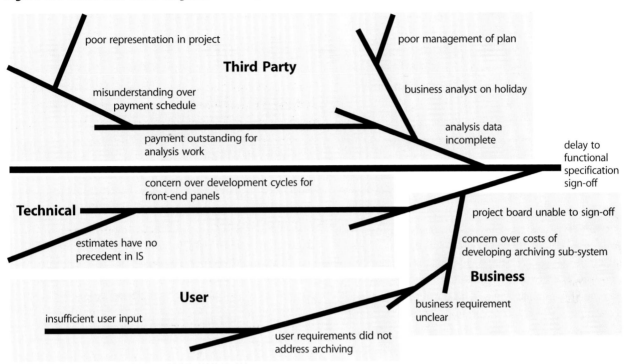

Brainstorming

The brainstorming process, borrowed from business management and not specifically created for risk management, involves redefining the problem, generating ideas, finding possible solutions, developing selected feasible solutions and conducting evaluation. The effectiveness of brainstorming is derived from two essential components: group thinking is more productive than individual thinking, and the avoidance of criticism improves the production of ideas. Ideas generated by one individual tend to trigger suggestions from other group members. Although widely used, the process does have its limitations. The sessions can be monopolised by dominant personalities and where criticism does occur it can be very corrosive.

Nominal Group Technique

The Nominal Group Technique is based on the silent generation of ideas by each individual, who then presents a single idea that is recorded but not discussed. Once all ideas have been recorded they are discussed and agreed. This technique overcomes the shortcomings of brainstorming, which can succumb to the influence of a few individuals who dominate idea discussion and generation. Research has shown this technique to be more productive than brainstorming in terms of the number of ideas generated, their uniqueness, and their quality.

Delphi Technique   *(oracle)*

Delphi is perhaps the best-known method of using group judgements in forecasting. It is a method for the systematic collection and collation of judgements from isolated anonymous respondents on a particular topic, through a set of carefully designed sequential questionnaires interspersed with summarised information and feedback of opinions derived from the earlier responses. The anonymity and isolation of respondents provides freedom from conformity pressures. In addition, the simple pooling of independent ideas and judgements facilitates equal participation of the respondents.

Risk questionnaire

A risk questionnaire aims to elicit through a series of questions, issues that are unresolved, incomplete, giving rise for concern, behind schedule, uncoordinated, appear to be in a rapid state of change or uncertain. A risk questionnaire can be structured in a number of ways. The objective is to draw out as much information as possible while at the same time not deterring the recipients from responding. The questionnaire should be structured in a logical manner to reflect a project lifecycle, process map or a similar structure, so that the recipients will immediately understand and be able to relate to it.

Table B.1 Database fields

Risk ID	Risk event	WBS
Date of entry	Probability	Business function
Status of the risk	Effect (cost)	RBS element
Originator	Effect (time)	Risk response category
Owner	Effect (business activity)	Risk action
Actionee	Risk date	Cost of response
Risk category	Project	Indicator
Cause	Phase	Trigger

Risk database

A risk database has a number of benefits. A newly constructed database can be used to capture information in a controlled and consistent way. Depending on its construction, its availability on a computer network, and the access rights established, it can permit multiple users to enter data or view the current information held. Some of the fields that a database would commonly hold are listed in Table B.1. Databases provide an audit trail of identification, assessment and implementation of management actions. Where risk information is collected on the completion of a project as part of a lessons learned study, it can be used to inform subsequent projects. This is accomplished by recording the risks that materialised, how they were addressed, budget and outturn costs, contingency allocation and spend, and achievement against objectives.

Gap analysis

Gap analysis can be used to draw out the main risks to an activity and is commonly carried out by calling on department heads to complete a questionnaire. An extract of a sample questionnaire is included in Figure B.5.

The questionnaire calls for an assessment to be made as to the current status of an activity in terms of how well it has been completed to date. The questionnaire identifies the two extremes in terms of the worst (column headed '1') and the best/perfect (column headed '5') position for the project. Recipients of the questionnaire are requested to score each row/line item inserting an 'X' in the column denoting their perception of the current activity position and a 'Y' in the column denoting the realistically achievable position. Recipients of the questionnaire are required to comment on all issues (as far as possible). If they are unable to comment on an item they are requested to place an 'N' in column 1 indicating that they have insufficient knowledge to comment on this activity/issue.

The meaning behind the columns headed 1 to 5 in Figure B.5 is explained in Figure B.6.

Figure B.5 Structure of questionnaire

Ref	Process	Issue	Worst Condition	1	2	3	4	5	Best Condition
5.1	Planning	Organisation	Decision-making process and its requirements (within the client organisation) not clearly communicated		X			Y	Decision-making process and its requirements clearly communicated

Figure B.6 Definition of categories of risk

1	**2**	**3**	**4**	**5**
Activity not commenced/ undertaken	Activity commenced but in outline only	Activity partially completed	Activity almost complete	Activity completed satisfactorily
Critical risk	Major risk	Significant risk	Minor risk	No risk to the project

B5 TECHNIQUES FOR THE ASSESS – ESTIMATE STEP

The Estimate step is concerned with assessing the likelihood of threat and opportunity events materialising and their respective impact should they materialise. The techniques used for this step are all about aiding the way we select, describe and communicate these assessment measures.

Pareto analysis

Pareto analysis is used to focus management effort on those risks that have the potential to have the greatest detrimental impact on an activity or an organisation's objectives. Pareto analysis is the expression given to the simple process of ranking or ordering risks once they have been assessed to determine the order in which they should be managed. The OGC states: 'it is important to focus on the most important risks – follow the Pareto principle of placing emphasis on and allocating resources to the significant few rather than the insignificant many' (PFI Material, Appendix B, Frequently Asked Questions and Common Problems, 2003).

Probability impact grid

Figure B.7 shows a probability impact grid containing ranking values that may be used to qualitatively rank previously identified risks. The probability scales are measures of probability derived from percentages. The impact scales have been selected subjectively to all be less than one. A banding can be applied to the qualitative assessments where any value at or over 0.18 is high priority, any value at or over 0.05 is medium priority, and any value below 0.05 is low priority. Qualitative words or quantitative data may be used to label the axes. Alternative scoring systems may be used for specific applications. These have the effect of changing the relative importance of risks.

The scales used in Fig B.7 are for illustrative purposes only. Alternative scales for probability can be found in Tables 3.1, 3.2 and 3.3. Alternative scales for impact can be found in Tables 3.4, 3.5 and 3.6.

Risk map

A simple form of qualitative risk estimation requires that the probability of a risk occurring is classified as, at a minimum: low (L), medium (M), or high (H) – with a similar classification for the impact if the risk materialises. A combined risk classification of 'H-H' (high probability and high impact if the risk occurs) is clearly an important risk. The classification can be extended to include very low and very high.

Figure B.7 Example of probability impact grid illustrating possible ranking values

Probability							
0.9	Very High 71-90%	0.045	0.09	0.18	0.36	0.72
0.7	High 51-70%	0.035	0.07	0.14	0.28	0.56
0.5	Medium 31-50%	0.025	0.05	0.10	0.20	0.40
0.3	Low 11-30%	0.015	0.03	0.06	0.12	0.24
0.1	Very Low up to 10%	0.005	0.01	0.02	0.04	0.08
		Very Low	Low	Medium	High	Very High
		0.05	0.1	0.2	0.4	0.8
		Impact				

Figure B.8 Risk map

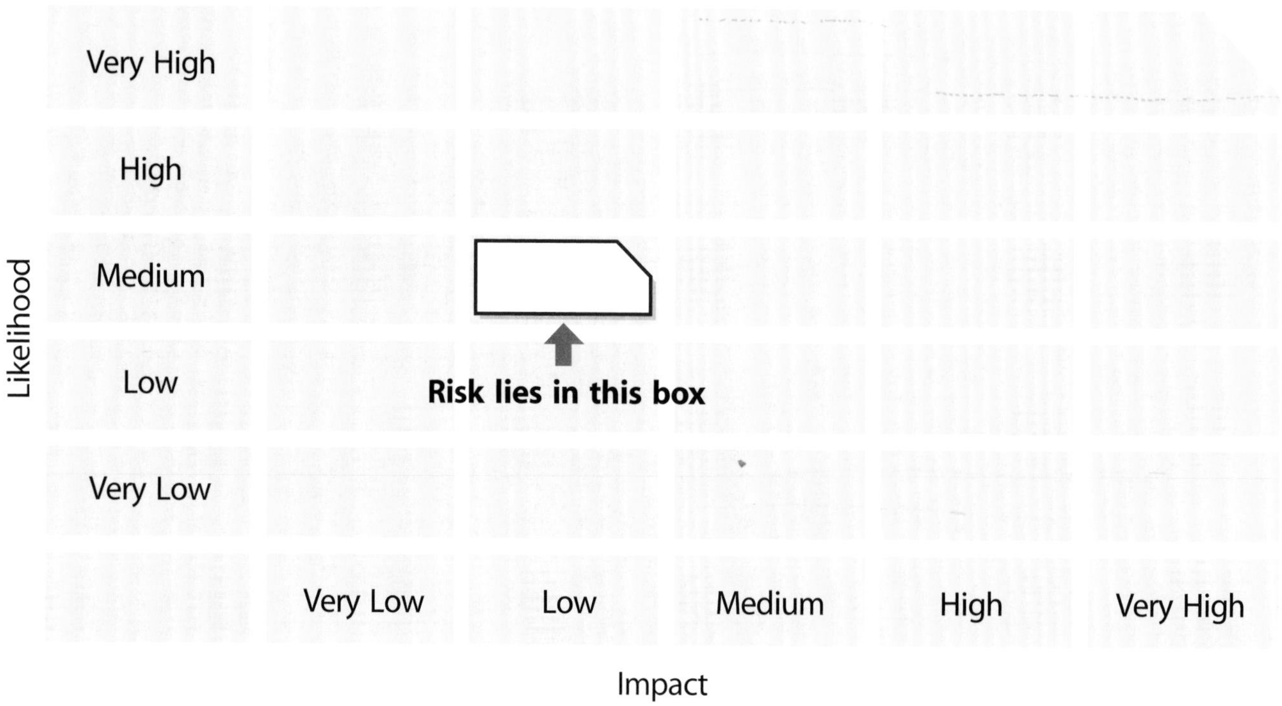

The precise meanings of the classifications must be stated before probability and impact estimations can be made. If this is not done, the terms tend to mean different things to different people.

The ranges should be selected to suit the situation, and take into consideration the business sensitivity. If the qualitative estimates are given explicit meaning in this way, boundaries between these classifications can be drawn to a scale and illustrated by the dividing lines on a risk map, as shown in Figure B.8.

Summary Risk Profile

A Summary Risk Profile must be used by all central government projects where there is an IT component. This is a simple mechanism to increase the visibility of risks; it is a graphical representation of information normally found on an existing Risk Register. In some industry sectors it is referred to as a risk map. The project manager or risk manager needs to update the Risk Register on a regular basis and then regenerate the graph, showing risks in terms of probability and impact with the effects of mitigating action taken into account. The Summary Risk Profile (see Figure B.9) shows all key risks as one picture, so that managers can gain an overall impression of the total exposure to risk. It is essential for the graph to reflect current information as documented in the Risk Register. The profile must be used with extreme care and should not mislead the reader. If an activity has over 200 risks it

will be impractical to illustrate all of the risks. It will be more appropriate to illustrate the top 20 risks, for example, making it clear what is and is not illustrated.

A key feature of this picture is the risk tolerance line, indicated here as a bold line. It shows the overall level of risk that the organisation is prepared to tolerate in a given situation. If exposure to risk is above this line, managers can see that they must take prompt action such as upward referral of relevant risks. Setting the risk tolerance line is a task for experienced risk managers; it reflects the organisation's attitudes to risk in general and to a specific set of risks within a particular project. The parameters of the risk tolerance line should be agreed at the outset of an activity and regularly reviewed.

The use of RAGB status can be useful for incorporating the status reporting from Risk Registers into risk profiles, and can provide a quick and effective means of monitoring (see Table B.2).

Figure B.9 Summary Risk Profile

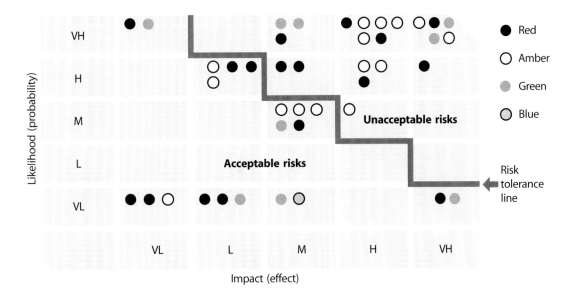

Table B.2 Expanding RAG status for reporting

Colour	Status
None	The risk management action cannot begin until a future specified date, therefore it is not possible to measure progress.
Red	No progress has been made.
Amber	Moderate progress is being made on risk management action, with little/no evidence of the deliverable.
Green	Progress is being made, commensurate with the stage of the project, with appropriate evidence of the deliverable.
Blue	Risk management action has been successfully completed and any associated deliverable has been provided.

CRAMM

CRAMM is a risk tool. It is a formal risk analysis and management methodology originally developed by the CCTA (now part of the OGC) in collaboration with a number of private sector organisations. CRAMM has been completely redeveloped by Insight Consulting to become a total information security toolkit that includes:

- A comprehensive risk assessment tool that is fully compliant with BS7799 and ISO 27001
- A range of help tools to support information security managers in planning and managing security
- Wizards to rapidly create pro-forma information security policies and other related documentation
- Tools that support the key processes in business continuity management
- A database of over 3000 security controls referenced to relevant risks and ranked by effectiveness and cost
- Essential tools to help achieve certification or compliance with BS7799.

Probability trees

Probability trees are graphical representations of possible events resulting from various circumstances. Construction of the probability tree usually commences from a single premise and works towards a series of possible outcomes.

Figure B.10 gives an example of how a probability tree might be constructed to assess the events leading to the impact of a dependent project overrunning (i.e. the impact on Project B when Project A overruns). Note that it is possible to calculate separately the probability of each event occurring and express this as a percentage or factor of 1.

In Figure B.10, Project B is dependent on the release of resources from Project A. Project A is overrunning. Depending on the outcome of possible actions relating to the termination of Project A, the probability of the resources being released can be estimated. Note the various actions available that can influence the outcome.

Figure B.10 Example of a probability tree

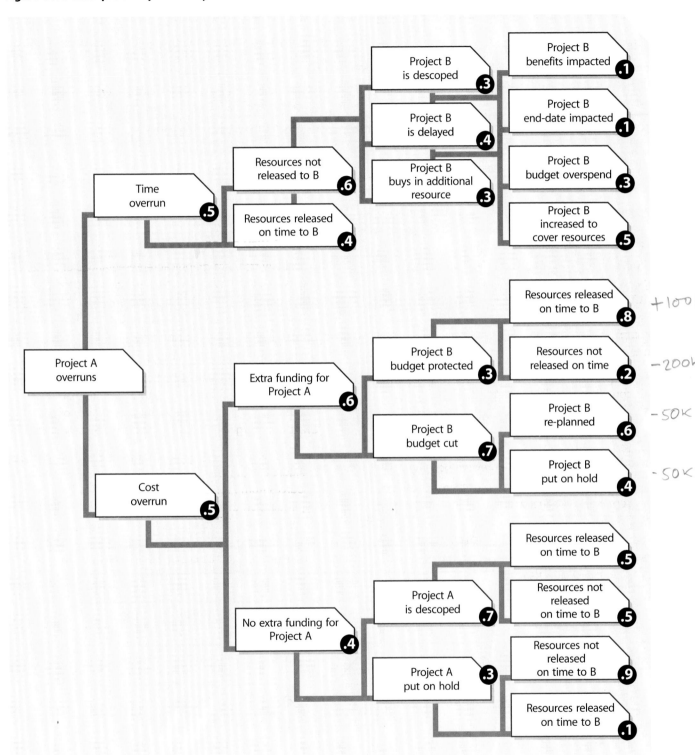

Expected value

The expected value is useful when a tangible measure of risk significance is required together with a need to prioritise risks. The approach is most effective when providing a measurement of the benefit of risk reduction gained through team consensus in a workshop as opposed to the judgement of an individual.

The approach quantifies risk by combining the cost of the risk impact with the probability of the risk occurring. The simplest form of calculation to employ is:

$CoI * P\% = EV$

where CoI is the estimated cost of the risk impact, P the probability of the impact occurring, and EV the expected value.

Table B.3 looks at the effect on expected value when using both experienced and inexperienced personnel. Three criteria for evaluation have been selected: the level of staff skill; staff availability; and the degree of staff control. Assumptions concerning each of these have been estimated against the cost of impact and the probability of impact.

The result in Table B.3 shows that the expected value for the risk is lessened by using experienced staff. A change in data for just one assumption, however, could reverse the result.

B6 TECHNIQUES FOR THE ASSESS – EVALUATE STEP

The Evaluate step is concerned with calculating the net effect of all of the threats and opportunities included on the Risk Register or a specific subset on the activity under examination. The techniques used for this step are typically associated with simulation techniques and displaying the results obtained.

Model

A model is simply a representation of a real business situation. Modelling involves a transformation process where outcomes are explained by a range of inputs and assumptions. Risk management models are used to capture our thinking, represent and more effectively analyse the aggregate effect of the threats and opportunities recorded on a Risk Register. They can be used to represent a wide variety of situations. As risk management models contain elements of uncertainty they are referred to as probabilistic or stochastic models. If reliance is to be placed on model results, however, a structured approach is required.

The construction has to be managed and the process needs to be reflective to ensure there is understanding between inputs to the model and the results obtained.

Table B.3 Example of a table showing the expected value method

Using experienced contract staff versus own inexperienced staff								
Risk	Cost of impact		X	Probability of impact		=	Expected value	
	Experienced	Inexperienced		Experienced	Inexperienced		Experienced	Inexperienced
Degree of skill								
Higher quality; repairs less likely	1.5m	1.5m		20%	60%		0.3m	0.9m
Higher fees; increased costs	0.25m	0.10m		100%	100%		0.25m	0.10m
Staff availability								
Faster completion; less likely to lose benefits this year	1.2m	1.2m		30%	90%		0.40m	1.08m
Degree of control								
Less likely to have a thorough understanding of the business	0.8m	0.8m		70%	30%		0.56m	0.24m
TOTALS							**£1.51m**	**£2.32m**

The old adage still applies: rubbish in, rubbish out. The quality of the output will be a direct result of the suitability and validity of the probability and impact assessment of each of the threats and opportunities. It will also be influenced by the choice of probability distribution selected to represent each variable (threat or opportunity) and the understanding of and the use of equations used to describe the relationship between each of the variables.

Simulation

Simulation is a technique that is helpful in analysing cost or time models, where the values of the input data, the variables, may be uncertain. Variables in this context refer to threats, opportunities, costs or durations. Simulation is possible with the aid of commercially available spreadsheet or programme software. The objective of simulation is to obtain a probability distribution of the likely outcome of an activity, when considering the input variables in combination. The thinking behind simulation is similar to the idea of carrying out multiple manual 'what if' scenarios. In a 'what if' analysis, a manager changes the values of selected input variables in a model to see what happens to the bottom-line performance figure/measure.

The difference between simulation and a manual 'what if' analysis is that the process of assigning values to variables within the cells in a spreadsheet is automated so that (1) the values are selected in a non-biased way and (2) the spreadsheet user is relieved of the burden of determining the values. Within simulation, sample values for each uncertain input variable are randomly and repeatedly generated and added to the model, and then the bottom-line performance measure (commonly a cost or duration) is calculated.

The performance measure results can be presented as a cumulative frequency curve or density graphs. The results provide a range of values, over which the performance measure might vary, to estimate its mean and variance and the probability that the actual value of the performance measure will be greater than or less than a particular value. All these measures provide greater insight into the risk associated with a given decision than a single value calculation based on the expected values for the uncertain variables.

Percentiles

A simulation will provide a series of values (or a number of possible outcomes) for a business activity. These results can be divided into equal parts. A series of values can be subdivided into two equal parts around the median. The median is the middle value of an ordered set of data (listing output values by size).

The concept of dividing the data into two equal parts can be extended to divide the data into quartiles, which is four equal parts. Quartiles of an ordered set of data are such that 25% of the observations are less than or equal to the first quartile (Q1), 50% are less than or equal to the second quartile (Q2), and 75% are less than or equal to the third quartile (Q3).

A series of values may also be subdivided into a greater number of equal parts such as deciles and percentiles, which divide the data into 10 and 100 parts, respectively. Although percentiles can be calculated manually, they are commonly generated by Monte Carlo simulation tools to provide confidence levels in the likely outturn cost of an investment, for example. An 80% confidence figure represents an 80% chance that the cost of the investment will be at this figure or less.

Monte Carlo simulation

Monte Carlo simulation refers to the traditional technique for using random numbers to sample from a probability distribution. The term Monte Carlo was introduced during World War II as a code name for simulation problems associated with development of the atomic bomb (Palisade 2002). Monte Carlo looks at a large number of 'what if' scenarios – for the financial outcome of a business activity, for example – by accounting for a large number of possible values that each variable could take and weighting each value by the probability of occurrence.

More specifically, the Monte Carlo simulation for cost models generates a number at random for each risk and cost item within the constraints of the probability distribution assigned to it (commonly triangular or rectangular/uniform) and weights this number in accordance with the probability of the risk occurring. These weighted random numbers are then aggregated to create one model simulation (iteration, trial or scenario), which is one possible value for the business activity. (So, for example, if a risk was assigned a uniform distribution with lower and upper limits of £15 and £30, respectively, and a probability of occurrence of 50%, then every other iteration would include the risk with a value assigned of between £15 and £30.) This value is then stored. This value (number) is one realistic outcome for the activity. The process is then repeated, commonly over 1000 times to give 1000 realistic possible outcomes for the activity.

We are concerned that the model will reproduce the distributions that have been included in the model. The only way that this can be achieved is by generating a large number of iterations. The statistical data describing each iteration is then aggregated and represented graphically by a histogram to show the range of possible outcomes, a probability distribution to illustrate possible skew and a cumulative frequency curve to show the likelihood (as a percentage) of exceeding the business objective (typically a finance limit).

Latin hypercube

Latin hypercube sampling is a more recent sampling technology than Monte Carlo. It is designed to accurately recreate the probability distributions specified by distribution functions in fewer iterations than the Monte Carlo sampling.

Latin hypercube creates a cumulative probability distribution curve for each variable. The significant difference between Latin hypercube and Monte Carlo is that Latin hypercube adopts stratified sampling of the input probability distributions. The process of stratification divides the cumulative frequency curve of each input into equal intervals on the cumulative probability scale of 0 to 1.0. A sample is then taken from each interval or stratification of the input distribution. Sampling is forced to represent values in each interval and is forced, therefore, to recreate the input probability distribution. The number of stratifications of the cumulative distribution is equal to the number of iterations performed. A sample is taken from each stratification. Once a sample is taken from a stratification, this stratification is not sampled again. Now that the speed and memory of both laptop and desktop computers has increased, the use of Latin hypercube sampling instead of Monte Carlo has diminished.

Critical path analysis or critical path method

Critical path analysis (CPA) or critical path method (CPM) models and associated software are useful for any form of activity planning. The CPA model represents activities using a network diagram. This approach is used to identify those activities that are dependent on another, for example, where one activity cannot start until one or more other activities have finished. All activities have assumed deterministic durations. Some activities can take place concurrently in order to identify where slippage will have an impact or where it will erode tolerance or require contingency actions.

Sensitivity analysis

Sensitivity analysis is the study of how varying one input in a model alters the model outcome. Another use of sensitivity analysis is to identify the input probability distributions that are significant in determining model

results. Sensitivity is usually carried out using Commercial Off The Shelf (COTS) software. Software typically employs the rank correlation calculation technique to determine, calculate and display the most significant inputs.

Cash flow analysis

Cash flow analysis provides additional information over and above profit and loss accounts and balance sheets. The main difference between a cash flow statement and a profit and loss account relates to the issue that profit is not the same as the increase in cash over a given accounting period, but rather is only one source of funds. Shareholders find cash flow analysis easier to understand than profit and loss accounts and balance sheets. Cash flow analysis provides more meaningful comparisons of performance over time. It provides information that facilitates an evaluation of the efficiency with which cash has been generated and used.

Portfolio analysis

Portfolio analysis is an extension of classical investment analysis and is aimed at dealing with risk. Portfolio analysis is used to put together a collection of investments with the lowest overall risks and the highest returns. The indicators of the risk associated with a portfolio include the volatility of the securities, the degree of positive correlation between the securities, and the variability in the rate of return. Each investment included within a portfolio needs to be carefully selected.

Cost-benefit analysis

Cost-benefit analysis is a procedure that takes into account all the costs and benefits (such as social benefits and costs). Its purpose is to give guidance in economic decision-making. Governments use it to evaluate important investment projects. The procedure places emphasis on externalities that would be completely ignored in a pure free market.

Using the construction of a toll road around a city as an example, the cost-benefit analysis would have to model the dis-benefits to local residents in terms of noise and air pollution, the destruction of areas of natural beauty and the loss of countryside recreational facilities. The analysis would also have to assess the time saved by the travellers using the motorway, the lives saved by taking traffic away from minor roads, any reduction in congestion and the improved business performance of commercial enterprises that use the motorway on a regular basis.

Assigning a value to the externalities is difficult, however. Cost-benefit analysis can be a very imprecise procedure. It is difficult to place a value on certain important costs and benefits and the results are critically dependent on the discount rate allowed for future costs applied to the calculations. At a lower level, cost-benefit analysis can be used to determine which risk response actions are the most beneficial.

Markov chain

A Markov chain combines the ideas of probability with those of matrix algebra. A matrix is a rectangular array of numbers arranged in rows and columns and is characterised by its size (or order), written as: (number of rows x number of columns). The whole matrix is usually referred to by a capital letter, whilst individual numbers, or elements, within the matrix are referred to by lower case letters, usually with a suffix to identify in which row and in which column they appear. Note that a matrix does not have a numerical value; it is merely a convenient way of representing an array of numbers.

The Markov chain concept assumes that probabilities remain fixed over time, but the system that is being modelled is able to change from one state to another, using these fixed variables as transition probabilities.

Utility theory

Utility theory assumes that every decision-maker uses a utility function that translates each of the possible payoffs in a decision problem into a non-monetary measure known as utility. The utility of a payoff represents the desirability (total worth or value) of the outcome of a decision alternative to the decision-maker. Different decision-makers have different attitudes and preferences towards risk and return. Those who are risk neutral tend to make decisions using the maximum EMV decision rule. Some decision-makers, however, are risk avoiders or are risk averse, and others look for risk or are risk seekers. Practitioners have experienced difficulty in implementing utility theory, and its usefulness and relevance has been called into question.

B7   TECHNIQUES FOR THE PLAN STEP

The Plan step is concerned with translating risk assessment and evaluation information into actions. Where risks relate to adverse events, responses should be implemented to reduce their effect, where the reduction effort or cost does not exceed the value of the risk. Where the intention is to maximise identified opportunities, the cost of capitalising on the opportunity should not exceed the likely value of the improvement. Techniques (or methods) used in this

step are aimed at risk efficiency. For a threat, the responses are shown in Chapter 3, Table 3.7.

For an opportunity, the responses are shown in Chapter 3, Table 3.10.

B8   TECHNIQUES FOR THE IMPLEMENT STEP

The primary goals of the Implement step are: ensuring that the planned responses have been implemented; understanding if they have been successful; assessing any residual risk where responses have not been totally successful; managing residual risk and managing new emerging threats and opportunities. The techniques used for this step are normally associated with measuring successful implementation.

Risk indicators

The risk indicator is the level of acceptability of a risk. Determining the risk indicator is a technique that can be used as part of the risk planning process prior to the evaluation activity.

The purpose of the risk indicator is to answer the question: do I need to do anything about the risk? It can be set as a threshold below or above which appropriate actions may be decided. The risk indicator is a filter to ensure that time is not wasted on risks that do not warrant further attention.

The risk indicator is often best expressed in terms of cost, i.e. the cost of implementing a risk response action or not. It may also be represented by a combination of time, cost and performance factors. In practice, the business sensitivity of the programme and the commercial environment will provide the necessary information to determine the levels of acceptability of risk.

Risks that are deemed to be unacceptable (that is, above the risk indicator) need to be managed proactively. Risks that fall within the limits of acceptability (that is, below the risk indicator) do not require any form of immediate action, although they should not be excluded from the ongoing monitoring process, since it is possible that a change of circumstances later may result in an acceptable risk becoming unacceptable.

Techniques for reporting

It is often useful to be able to present the results of risk analysis in a simple way. Risk maps, radar charts, histograms and scatter diagrams are typical examples. The choice of presentation must be tailored to suit the reporting requirements of the board, programme or project.

Radar chart

A radar chart has a strong visual impact (it is also known as a spider web chart). Figure B.11 is a very simple example of a radar chart that has been used to show the number of risks that five different projects are exposed to. Initially the data is placed in a table that is subsequently converted into a chart using proprietary software. In a radar chart, a point close to the centre on any axis indicates a low value. A point near the edge is a high value.

Scatter diagram

A scatter diagram can be created using a similar scale to that of a probability impact grid, but showing concentrations of risk represented by groups of dots. The benefit of such a diagram is to show more visually where the concentrations of risk are greatest. Figure B.12 shows an example of a scatter diagram.

Figure B.12 Scatter diagram

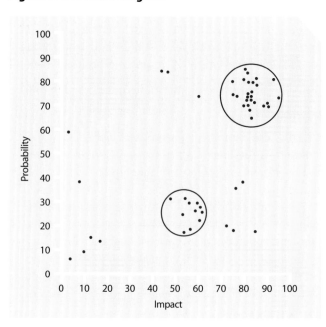

Figure B.11 Radar chart

Project	Number of risks
Project A	52
Project B	68
Project C	42
Project D	100
Project E	12

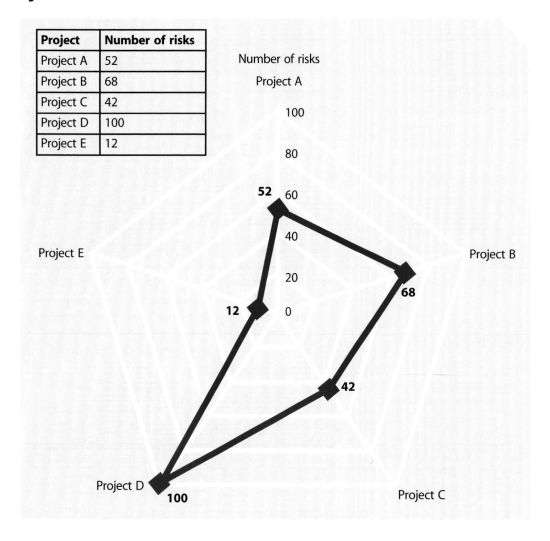

B9 SUMMARY

Table B.6 provides a schedule of the techniques described in this appendix and the risk process steps where it is suggested that they are applied.

Table B.6 A range of typical techniques and the risk activity for which they are best suited

Technique	Identify – Context	Identify – Identify the risks	Assess – Estimate	Assess – Evaluate	Plan	Implement
Project lifecycle	✓					
Process map	✓					
PEST	✓					
SWOT	✓					
RACI	✓					
Stakeholder matrix	✓					
Project Profile Model		✓				
Risk checklist		✓				
Risk prompt list		✓				
Lessons learned logs		✓				
Risk breakdown structure		✓				
Risk taxonomy		✓				
Risk identification workshop		✓				
Cause and effect diagrams		✓				
Brainstorming		✓				
Nominal group technique		✓				
Delphi Technique		✓				
Risk questionnaire		✓				
Risk database		✓				
Gap analysis		✓				
Pareto analysis			✓			
Probability impact grid			✓			
Risk map			✓			
Summary Risk Profile			✓			
Probability trees			✓			
Expected value			✓			
CRAMM			✓			
Models				✓		
Simulation				✓		
Percentiles				✓		
Monte Carlo simulation				✓		

Table B.6 A range of typical techniques and the risk activity for which they are best suited (continued)

Technique	Identify – Context	Identify – Identify the risks	Assess – Estimate	Assess – Evaluate	Plan	Implement
Latin hypercube				✓		
Critical path analysis				✓		
Sensitivity analysis				✓		
Cash flow analysis				✓		
Portfolio analysis				✓		
Cost-benefit analysis				✓		
Markov chain				✓		
Utility theory				✓		
Reduction					✓	
Removal					✓	
Transfer					✓	
Retention					✓	
Share					✓	
Realisation					✓	
Enhancement					✓	
Exploitation					✓	
Risk indicators						✓
Radar charts						✓
Scatter diagram						✓

Management of risk healthcheck

Appendix C: Management of risk healthcheck

C1 PURPOSE

Good risk management practice occurs when the management of risk principles have been well applied. The management of risk healthcheck is a tool for checking the health of current risk management and for identifying areas where its application might be improved. It may be used for self-assessment, peer review or external assessment.

The healthcheck is most useful when preparing and carrying out an enterprise-wide assessment. It is also applicable for assessments of specific programmes, projects or operational activities. This healthcheck is only a starting point. It should be adapted to the particular assessment and nature of the business.

The healthcheck might prove useful:

- When considering a new investment such as a major programme or project
- As an integral part of business planning activity
- When preparing to establish commitment to improving risk management
- Before or as complement to a gateway review
- When developing an annual operational plan.

C2 PROCESS

To be effective, the healthcheck should be formally administered and repeated to monitor changes over time. Each administration of the healthcheck will occur using the following steps:

Preparation

- Define the terms of reference (scope, timing, etc.) based on the sponsor's needs
- Define the roles and responsibilities
- Select a review team
- Collect background information for the team
- Brief the team and share background information
- Refine the healthcheck approach
- Refine the question set (using the questions below as a starting point)
- Define the necessary interviews
- Schedule interviews (as appropriate).

Data collection

- Review written documentation (as appropriate) and note individual findings
- Conduct interviews (as appropriate) and document findings from each.

Data analysis

- Identify trends and patterns
- Note deficiencies
- Note strengths
- Identify three to five key themes
- Conduct intermediate review with the sponsor
- Identify recommendations.

Review and report

- Draft report
- Conduct final review with the sponsor
- Finalise report.

C3 FRAMEWORK

The healthcheck assesses risk management practice. It is recommended that the 12 management of risk principles be used as a framework for structuring the assessment.

Figure C.1 Management of risk principles

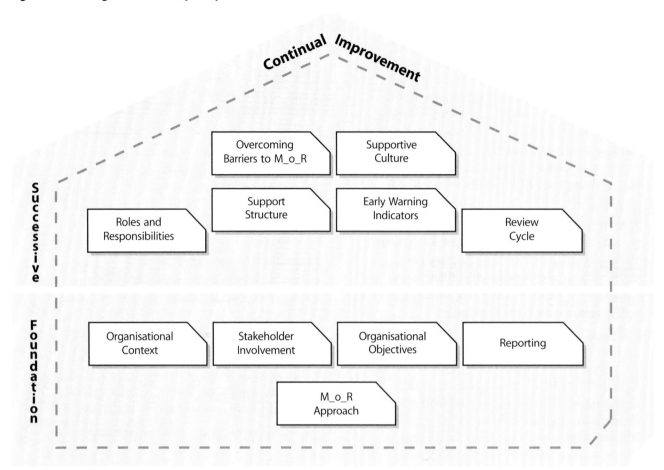

Each principle listed below is followed by a set of questions. An affirmative response identifies an aspect of the principle that has been applied; a negative response identifies a lack of comprehensive application of the principles. The more questions that are answered in the affirmative, the closer the application of risk management approaches good practice.

It is important to answer the questions realistically. Improvement will not result from being overly optimistic or answering questions the way they 'ought' to be answered. It is advisable that an objective third party leads or, as a minimum, participates in the assessment. The third party may be an internal auditor, an external auditor, an independent consultant, a member of another risk management team or, as a minimum, a peer who is not directly involved with the work under assessment.

Within the healthcheck questions set below, the term Risk Management Policy is used. This is meant to represent a single or collection of policies as appropriate to the nature of the organisation.

Organisational context

Consideration: the management of risk should reflect the context of the organisation and the nature of the organisational activity under examination.

■ Has external analysis of the organisation, programme, project or operation under examination been conducted (e.g. using PESTLE analysis, industry analysis, scenario planning or environmental scanning)?

■ In the external analysis, have key organisations been explicitly identified and considered?

■ Is the external analysis fully documented?

■ Has the complexity of the risk environment been ascertained as part of a formal process (e.g. completing a risk potential assessment)?

■ Has the capability and capacity of the organisation to accommodate the complexity of the risk environment been assessed?

■ Have a range of risk identification approaches appropriate to the external environment been adopted?

■ Have contractual, legal and regulatory compliance been considered?

- Is there a clearly defined process for monitoring and reassessment of contextual risks in place? Has a future review of the analysis been scheduled?
- Have the internal capabilities (e.g. process, technology, skills) required to respond to external risks been identified?
- Have the inherent types of risk – threats and opportunities – associated with the context been categorised and described? Are these communicated?
- Is there a preliminary definition of who (or which part of the organisation) will own certain categories of risk in the first instance?
- Have risks that are on the horizon (i.e. emerging and perhaps not fully understood) been considered as well as those that are immediate and well understood?
- Is risk management integrated into key planning activities (e.g. business planning, business case development, project initiation, operational planning and portfolio management)?
- Does a Risk Management Policy exist? Does it explicitly describe how it reflects the organisational context?
- Has contextual analysis and risk identification been reviewed and constructively challenged by the board, senior responsible owner (or equivalent), and risk manager (as appropriate)?
- Have specialists been engaged if necessary and as appropriate?
- Has a risk appetite for the organisation, programme, project or operation under examination been identified?

Stakeholder involvement

Consideration: the management of risk should involve all major stakeholders.

- Have the major stakeholders who have an impact on or are affected by the objectives been identified?
- Have risks affecting stakeholders (and stakeholders influencing risks) been explicitly identified and evaluated?
- Where appropriate, have stakeholders been included in the identification and assessment of risk?
- Have stakeholders been provided with timely, specific and clear information about risks, particularly when a new major activity is being proposed or objectives change?
- Have stakeholder objectives for an activity been captured, disseminated, discussed, aligned and agreed with any omissions being signed off?
- Have stakeholder perceptions and attitudes towards risk been identified? Is this documented and reviewed?

- Has the level of risk acceptable to stakeholders been debated or negotiated, as appropriate?
- Given stakeholder input, is there a clear definition of what level of strategic, programme, project and operational risk is acceptable?
- Is there a mechanism in place for funding the agreed level of risk? Has this mechanism also been discussed with stakeholders, as appropriate?
- Is there a process for eliciting stakeholder interests and identifying associated risk?
- Is there a mechanism for including stakeholder input into the identification and assessment of risk as appropriate?
- Has the organisation established a record of consistently avoiding the understatement or overstatement of high-profile risks?
- Have specialists been used if necessary?

Organisational objectives

Consideration: the management of risk should be undertaken against clear objectives.

- Have the objectives of the organisation or activity under examination been clearly documented in advance of risk identification?
- Has risk analysis been conducted relative to the organisation and activity objectives?
- Are objectives specific, measurable, achievable, relevant and time-bound (i.e. SMART)?
- Are objectives reviewed and updated in view of risks identified?
- Has management defined levels of acceptable risk to objectives?
- Does the management team regularly review the acceptable level of risk?
- Has the overall approach to risk management been reviewed when objectives have changed?
- Is there a process for monitoring changes to objectives and the impact on risk?
- Are changes to objectives considered and reflected in changes to the Risk Management Policy and Risk Management Strategies?
- Have the relationships and interdependencies between programme, project and operational objectives been considered?
- Are identified risks formally made available to the objective setting processes?
- Is the achievability of objectives reviewed when changes to the risk profile are identified?

M_o_R approach

Consideration: organisations should develop an approach to the management of risk that reflects its objectives.

- Is there an overarching Risk Management Policy governing risk management for the organisation under consideration?
- Does the Risk Management Policy clearly describe which activities should be routinely subject to risk management?
- Does the Risk Management Policy describe key risk management roles and responsibilities?
- Does the Risk Management Policy make explicit the organisation's risk appetite and risk bearing capacity?
- Does the Risk Management Policy accommodate different perspectives (strategic, programme, project and operational)?
- Does the Risk Management Policy accommodate the inherent categories/types of risk faced by the organisation?
- Has the Risk Management Policy been tested by the executive management team to see if it fully reflects the nature and extent of the risks facing the organisation? Has it been assured by a third party?
- Does a Risk Management Strategy exist for the activity under consideration (strategic, programme, project or operation)?
- Are appropriate tools and techniques that enhance the effectiveness of risk management readily available?
- Is there a formal approach to choosing appropriate tools and techniques that enhance the effectiveness of risk management?
- Are risks assessed in a way that enables risk management action to be prioritised and be as effective as possible?
- Is a procedure in place for identifying when risks have exceeded tolerances?
- Is there a pre-arranged channel for automatically escalating ownership of critical risks that exceed tolerances to more senior management for decision-making?
- Is there a process for delegating ownership of low-grade risks to more junior levels of management?
- Is there a process for reassigning risk ownership between programmes, projects and operational units?
- Does a Risk Register exist for the activity under consideration (organisation, programme, project or operational unit)?

- Does the Risk Register include a combination of the maximisation of opportunities and the mitigation of threats?
- Have specialists been used if necessary?

Reporting

Consideration: the governing body of organisations should receive, review and act on risk management reports.

Receive

- Has a regular risk reporting process been defined? Is it clear how it will be used, when and by whom? Is it clear who will create and disseminate reports?
- Have the managers receiving risk management reports agreed to the form and content?
- Is there a commonly understood and expedient path for risks to be escalated to senior levels of management if required?
- Does the programme, project or operational unit accommodate risk exception reporting? Alternatively, is there a process for fast-tracking regular reports if necessary?
- Are Risk Progress Reports sent to, and received from, other organisations, groups or partners that are worked with on a regular basis?
- Do reports make clear the interdependencies between organisational activities and the corresponding risk profile?
- Does the management team agree that the risk information required to support their necessary decision-making is communicated in a timely, clear and cost-effective manner?

Review

- Has the type of risk analysis required to support decision-making by governing bodies been agreed?
- Are risk reports succinct, accurate and focused, and do they include an executive summary for speed of assimilation?
- Do reports recommend actions as well as identify threat or opportunity considerations?
- Are actions that require prompt responses highlighted?
- Does the executive management team or senior responsible owner regularly assess the risk profile and the financial implications to the organisation, programme, project or operational units?
- Are the cross-impacts of risks from interdependent programmes, projects and operational units considered?

- Is there an agreed risk profile (e.g. a view on the high-, medium- and low-level risks) for the investment under consideration?

Act

- Does each governing body have a funding mechanism in place to finance risk responses, e.g. portfolio management, a contingency fund, new opportunity budget or controlled release of budgets to activities?
- Does each governing body have a mechanism for stopping, starting or rescoping work between planning cycles?
- Do senior executives report to stakeholders how key organisational risks and associated financial implications are being dealt with?
- Is the level of response commensurate with the level of risk?

Roles and responsibilities

Consideration: organisations should establish clear roles and responsibilities for the management of risk in terms of leadership, direction, controls, ongoing risk management, reporting and reviewing.

- Does the management board explicitly sponsor risk management? Is this communicated and demonstrated to staff?
- Are the skills and level of resources available appropriate for the area of concern?
- Is the internal audit function clearly separated from the risk management function in order to maintain impartiality?
- Is there clear ownership for the establishment and management of the Risk Management Policy and Risk Management Process Guide?
- Is there clear ownership of the Risk Management Strategy?
- Is there a centre of excellence and does it provide appropriate tools and techniques?
- Does the centre of excellence act as conduit for corporate risk reporting?
- Is the capability and capacity of the centre of excellence appropriate for the complexity of the organisation?
- Has there been a formal communication (by senior management) to all managers within the business about their risk management responsibilities?
- Is communication with managers regarding risk management maintained on a regular basis?

- Do all staff members understand that they have a role to play in risk management? Are specific responsibilities included in job descriptions?
- Is good risk management reinforced by line manager behaviours and reward systems? Does the formal system in place explicitly consider risk management?
- Are clear risk management roles defined for all organisational objectives (and therefore all key programmes, projects and operational activities)?
- Do staff members know to whom they should identify new risks or changes to existing risks?
- Are clear accountabilities and roles for risk management defined within partner organisations (extended relationships)?
- Is there assurance that individuals within partner organisations, who have been allocated ownership, actually have the authority and capability to fulfil their risk management responsibilities?
- Is risk ownership reassessed on a periodic basis or in the event of a change in context, and if necessary can it be quickly and effectively reallocated?
- Do individual risks and response actions have clearly identified owners? Do owners have the authority required?
- Are the nominated owners appropriate and aware of their nomination?
- Has there been a clear allocation of responsibilities for reviewing risk management in the organisation?
- Are non-executive members of the management board in place with responsibility for challenging risk assumptions and promoting good risk management practice?
- Are risks being allocated to the appropriate (senior or junior) level?
- Does the organisation make functional specialists (e.g. internal auditors, health and safety officers, financial officers or risk improvement managers) available where appropriate?
- Are specialists assigned to provide advice and support to the management team on policy, strategies plans and processes?

Support structure

Consideration: a structure to support the management of risk for the organisational activity under consideration should be established.

- Does a central risk function (e.g. portfolio office, programme office, project office or business office) exist for the organisational activity under consideration?
- Are dedicated individuals (part- or full-time) assigned to the central risk function?
- Are individuals independent of the audit activities?
- Do the roles in the central risk function have detailed role descriptions and appropriate performance management targets?
- Do personnel experienced in the discipline of risk management staff the central risk function?
- Is there an induction process for personnel joining the central risk function? Does the induction include familiarisation with all departments within the organisation, the regulatory context and all existing processes and procedures? Have all personnel within the central risk function been through such an induction?
- Are staff familiar with the business (i.e. its core activities, stakeholders and culture)?
- Is the central risk function formally linked to the risk management processes across the organisation?
- Does the central risk function have the mandate, skills profile and funding available to assess and improve risk in the organisation?
- Is there some form of risk profile management process in place (i.e. is it apparent that there is rigour in collecting risks together into a profile, comparing risks and actively balancing the types and level of risk)?

Early warning indicators

Consideration: organisations should establish early warning indicators for critical business activities as part of proactive risk management to provide information on the potential sources of risk.

- Are all critical business systems clearly defined? Do early warning indicators exist for critical business systems (i.e. operational)?
- Do early warning indicators exist for designated programmes and projects?
- Are there overall organisational early warning indicators (strategic)?

- Are strategic, programme and project early warning indicators linked into risk reporting processes for all critical business systems?
- Is there a balanced set of indicators, including financial indicators?
- Are indicators examined by decision-makers with the authority to take corrective action on a regular cycle?
- Are the reports presented in a concise, consistent manner so that the impact of the information is readily understood?
- Are the indicators changed as the business changes or the context of the business changes?
- Are the indicators inward and outward looking (i.e. do they measure changes in the organisation's environment)?
- Is the granularity of early warning indicators reviewed to ensure they are appropriate for the required decision-making?

Review cycle

Consideration: organisations should regularly review the risks the organisation is facing and the policies, processes, strategies and plans it is adopting to manage them.

- Is the management of the Risk Management Policy and processes reviewed on a regular cycle for its effectiveness?
- Is the effectiveness of risk responses monitored and reviewed?
- Is assurance provided to the management board that reviews are undertaken?
- Is assurance provided on the quality and objectivity of the review?
- Are findings of reviews reported to policy, process, strategy and plan owners?
- Is a process defined for scoping and conducting reviews?
- Are the structure, content and format of the review reports defined?
- Do reports highlight significant risks and the effectiveness of the response actions in managing those risks?
- Are significant control failings or weaknesses identified and discussed in the reports?
- Are the impacts of failings or weaknesses on the organisation discussed?
- Are the responses to failings and weaknesses that have been put in place discussed?

- Are reviews coordinated with the internal audit committee, the timing of annual reports and external inspections by a regulator and shareholder meetings?
- Are specialists being used optimally?

Overcoming barriers to M_o_R

Consideration: the management of risk should recognise and respond to the barriers to implementation.

- Do middle and junior managers believe senior management adequately supports risk management?
- Are formal risk management training, tools and techniques readily available for staff to use?
- Do staff members know how to access risk management training, tools and techniques?
- Are risk management training needs assessed regularly?
- Have staff members demonstrated that they are sufficiently aware of the importance of risk management?
- Are risk management orientation, induction and training processes in place for staff – including senior management and executives?
- Is there a standard process/procedure for addressing concerns with risk management tools or practices?
- Is an adequate budget for embedding and executing risk management available?
- Are effective practices, productive behaviours and investments in risk management identified and rewarded?
- Is there a corporate process for identifying good practices and documenting them?
- Are good practices shared across the organisation on a regular basis?
- Is there a uniform approach to processes and reporting to ensure the adoption of best practice and the ease of amalgamating information?

Supportive culture

Consideration: organisations should establish the right culture for supporting risk management throughout the organisation.

- Does a member of the management board own risk management?
- Are risk management processes linked directly to key planning activities (e.g. corporate planning, financial management, and programme and project initiation)?
- Is the level of resource applied to risk management commensurate with the level of risk to objectives?

- Is the rigour of assessment commensurate with the level of risk? For example, are detailed assessments of probabilities being avoided on threats that are known to have little or no impact?
- Does senior management demonstrate commitment (e.g. through its policy, level of effort and actions) to risk management?
- Does senior management foster a climate of trust so that risks can be openly shared and discussed without fear?
- Are staff rewarded and valued, rather than being blamed, for highlighting risks?
- Is there visibility of risk management and regular communication to staff regarding risk management topics?
- Does the organisation take time to assess the root causes of risks?
- Is there a code of conduct, human resource policy and a performance reward system to support risk management?
- Are competencies in risk management part of individual performance evaluation and critical to career progression?
- Are there tools in place for embedding risk management, e.g. e-learning, seminars, case studies, lessons learned and company exchanges?

Continual improvement

Consideration: organisations should develop strategies to improve their risk management maturity.

- Is there a person or team responsible for improving risk management for the organisation, programme, project or operation in question?
- Are practices reviewed against a maturity model to determine the level of maturity attained and the corresponding benefits that can be expected?
- Is there an improvement plan prepared for progression of the risk management practices from the current level to the next level in the maturity model?
- Prior to implementing the improvement plan, have the benefits to be obtained from reaching the next level of maturity been compared with the resources required to achieve the next level?
- Is the improvement plan being managed as a project with clear objectives, resources and timeframe?

Management of risk
maturity model

→ confidence that
things being done
right

Appendix D: Management of risk maturity model

D1 INTRODUCTION

The purpose of this appendix is to introduce the subject of maturity models, their use, composition and their benefits.

Maturity models are a valuable tool in enabling organisations to benchmark their current risk management capability and maturity and in understanding how and where improvement may be achieved. They are intended to provide a well-structured and detailed guide to facilitate the progressive incremental improvement in risk management practices. With the aid of a maturity model, organisations can set realistic long-term goals for risk management, by having a clear understanding of their current maturity (in terms of current working practices) and the areas that require improvement.

The use of maturity models is now widespread, with international adoption across multiple industries. They provide a direct way of enabling organisations to describe, communicate and implement process improvement. They contain the essential elements of effective processes and describe an evolutionary improvement path from ad hoc, immature processes to disciplined, mature processes with improved quality and effectiveness.

The 'parent' of the majority of maturity models is the Capability Maturity Model (CMM) published by the Software Engineering Institute (SEI) based at Carnegie Mellon University, Pittsburgh, US.

D2 PROCESS IMPROVEMENT

Continual learning organisations look to improve their processes to enhance their overall performance in an ever-changing and increasingly competitive environment. The benefits of risk management derived by organisations will depend directly on the level of maturity of their risk management practices.

In the absence of an organisation-wide knowledge infrastructure, however, repeatable results depend entirely on the availability of specific individuals with a proven track record, and this does not necessarily provide the basis for long-term success and continual improvement throughout an organisation.

As a result, organisations are increasingly turning to maturity models for assessing and improving processes on the premise that the quality of a system or product is highly influenced by the quality of the process used to develop and maintain it.

D3 DEFINITION

In general terms a risk maturity model is a generally accepted reference model or framework of mature practices for appraising an organisation's risk management competency. Experience has shown that risk management maturity can be described as a series of distinct incremental steps that progressively derive greater benefits. A maturity model is a structured collection of elements that describe characteristics of effective processes.

A maturity model provides:

- A starting point in terms of how we move forward
- A place to capture the organisation's previous experiences and current capabilities
- A common language
- A communication tool to succinctly describe the current status and what is possible
- A framework for prioritising actions
- A way of describing what improvement means specific to the organisation
- A shared goal.

D4 PURPOSE

The purpose of the management of risk maturity model is to enable organisations to determine by assessment their level of risk management maturity when measured against the criteria included in the model.

D5 SCOPE

The boundaries to a maturity model are defined by the ends of the continuum between the competencies of a novice process to the sophistication of a fully mature process achieving optimum benefits.

D6   STRUCTURE/COMPOSITION

As illustrated in Figure D.1, constructing a maturity model requires three types of information: a set number of levels of capability; criteria in the form of risk management practices; and competencies that describe specific capabilities.

Figure D.1 Inputs to a maturity model

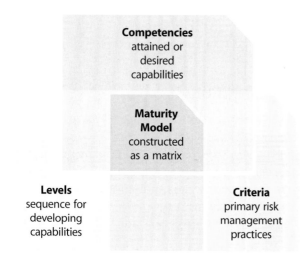

D7   LEVELS

Maturity models are typically composed of four or five levels of maturity and the quality of the processes within each level is described by the use of assessment criteria. There is no limit on the number of criteria that might be adopted, although models commonly contain fewer than 10 to avoid becoming unwieldy. The common structure for a maturity model is a matrix, as illustrated in Table D.1. On a completed matrix, each of the cells is populated with a competency.

The levels within a maturity model provide:

- Stepping stones for incremental improvement

- A realistic and sensible transitional route from an immature state to that of a mature and capable organisation
- A tool for the objective judgement of the quality of risk management practices.

Level labels

Each level is given a label and an overview or general description of what that level (of attainment) means. Examples of level labels adopted elsewhere are included in Table D.3 at the end of this appendix.

Description of the levels

When constructing a model it is necessary to define each of the levels in summary form, in terms of the degree of maturity of the risk management capabilities practised at that level. This helps organisations discern more quickly what their capabilities are and how realistically their organisation's processes can be classified.

D8   CRITERIA

The levels are aimed at describing a stage of development in implementing a practice. The criteria are primary risk management practices that an organisation would establish to develop risk management capabilities. These would typically be:

- Content of a risk management process
  - Identify – context and risks
  - Assess – estimate and evaluate
  - Plan
  - Implement.
- Applying the process
- Providing training to enable staff to understand and implement the process
- Management oversight of the process
- Embedding the process within the organisation.

Table D.1 Structure of a maturity model

	Level 1 Initial	Level 2 Repeatable	Level 3 Defined	Level 4 Managed	Level 5 Optimising
Criterion 1					
Criterion 2					
Criterion 3					
Criterion 4					
Criterion 5					
Criterion 6					

D9   COMPETENCIES

The competencies included in the cells of the matrix describe how well developed these practices should be for each of the different levels. For instance, the competencies will describe incremental improvements in risk identification across the different levels of a model.

D10   MANAGEMENT OF RISK MATURITY MODEL

Included below is an overview of the management of risk model. Initially the levels are described followed by a matrix of the levels and assessment criteria. The higher the level of risk maturity attained by an organisation, the greater its prospects for successfully managing risk and the lower its potential for failure. For any organisation, once the gap between its current state and desired state has been identified and documented, management must then evaluate the expected costs and benefits of increasing its risk management capabilities.

Description of the levels

The summary descriptions of levels included below define the different levels of maturity that represent incremental improvement until optimising behaviour is reached where there is a culture of continual improvement in risk management and all other internal controls.

Initial: The first level is where the organisation undertakes the minimum risk identification and assessment to satisfy compliance requirements and where risks to the organisation are examined on an annual or bi-annual basis. The organisation has not defined its risk tolerance/appetite, there is no formal risk process, and the sources of potential threat and opportunity have not been recorded and disseminated. Management actions are primarily reactive rather than proactive. Staff act on their own initiative to put out fires.

Repeatable: The second level is where a risk framework has been established that includes a definition of the organisation's risk tolerance/appetite, the risk management process, and when it will be applied. In addition there is an understanding of the risk profile in terms of the sources of risk facing the organisation and their likely impact. Resources are allocated to risk management efforts with specific individuals designated, with defined roles, responsibilities and authorities.

Defined: Risk management processes are further developed and refined. A central risk management function has been created coordinating effort, minimising duplication, creating an audit trail and ensuring a consistent approach. There is also a core of experienced individuals who are capable of modelling and response planning. Early warning indicators are developed for operational risk and business continuity plans are prepared. The board debate the high-level risks on a regular cycle and risk management is used to improve business performance.

Managed: The risk management culture is led by the CEO and risk management is routinely used by the organisation for decision-making. The additional improvements and increased sophistication at this higher level are primarily around improved quantification driven by more rigorous analysis. There is a stronger emphasis on measuring, aggregating and managing risks across the organisation. Risk measures are linked to performance goals. Additionally, early warning indicators and capital allocation techniques are effectively deployed.

Optimising: The optimising state is the highest level of maturity. There is a culture of continual improvement that improves on and develops the capabilities established at the prior levels. It is at this level that the organisation fully aligns its risk management policies, profile, process, framework and resources. A training and education programme is provided for all business unit heads. Risk management responsibilities are included in job descriptions, the staff induction process and performance appraisals. Proactive opportunity management is integrated within the risk management process and receives as much attention as downside risk.

Table D.2 Maturity model matrix

Criteria	Level 1 Initial	Level 2 Repeatable	Level 3 Defined	Level 4 Managed	Level 5 Optimising
Context of the organisation/ activity	Context of the organisation is not reflected in risk identification	Examination of the context is built into the risk process	Context is rigorously examined to explore both threats and opportunities	Managers proactively inform the central risk function of major changes in the context	The context is used to inform the M_o_R process, objective setting and opportunity management
Involve all major stakeholders	Not all stakeholders are consulted	Stakeholders are identified and engaged	Communication strategy is developed. Stakeholder objectives are identified, captured, aired, aligned, agreed and signed off	Fully documented processes. Clear process map of activities	Advance lobbying of stakeholders to encourage support and engagement very early in the investment cycle
Clear objectives	Activity objectives are not always made explicit prior to M_o_R activity	Threats are identified against explicit objectives	Objectives include stakeholder requirements	M_o_R is used to redefine objectives where appropriate as part of risk response planning	M_o_R is used to identify opportunities and influence objective setting
Policies, processes, strategies and plans	Undocumented or vague. No operating limits defined. No review of emerging risks or opportunities	Policies and process are defined. Risk tolerance levels are established. Timing of M_o_R is agreed	Policies are further developed, refined and disseminated. Central risk function is established	M_o_R is routinely used to support decision-making. Improved quantitative analysis	Enterprise-wide strategies. Focus is on continual improvement
Risk management reports	No formal periodic reporting	Basic management reports are issued consistently and in a timely manner	Senior management reports in a consistent format. Audit reports. Prioritised actions	Threshold limit violations are reported. Risk measurement linked to early warning indicators (EWIs). Contingency spend reported	Option analysis. Sensitivity analysis. Scenario modelling
Roles and responsibilities	Staff act on their own initiative in silos. No coordinated approach	Risk owners, managers and actionees are identified and risk actions assigned	Integrated teams across the organisation	Requisite knowledge, expertise and experience is in place	Organisation, processes, and individual performance measures are fully aligned
Central risk function	No central point of contact for guidance or direction	Roles and responsibilities of central risk function are established	Relationship with the internal audit committee, the board and divisions is developed	Embedding risk management, 'selling' the benefits and refining the process	Driving improvements, integrating across divisions and aiding opportunity management

Table D.2 Maturity model matrix (continued)

Criteria	Level 1 Initial	Level 2 Repeatable	Level 3 Defined	Level 4 Managed	Level 5 Optimising
Early warning indicators (EWIs)	EWIs are not established	EWIs are identified and monitored	EWIs are refined and trends included in M_o_R reports	EWIs are used to inform M_o_R management and decision-making	EWIs are used for proactive management and opportunity seeking
Review the effectiveness of processes	No formal processes. Reactionary ad hoc responses. Compliance focused	Process gaps are identified, assessed and corrected	Uniform processes are adopted across the organisation	Risk management is fully integrated with line management	Continual benchmarking. Best practices are identified and shared across the organisation
Barriers to implementation	Barriers not recognised	Common barriers are recognised and addressed	Roles and responsibilities are refined across the organisation	M_o_R is championed by CEO	Risk is embedded in the organisation in terms of job descriptions, induction, appraisals and performance targets
Risk culture	No defined policy, profile, process or vocabulary. No defined risk appetite	Risk appetite, profile and process defined	EWIs established	Risk appetite regularly reviewed and communicated. Process updated as the result of feedback	Refined risk appetite. Strident initiatives to establish and maintain best practice
Strategies for improving risk management maturity	No risk management training. Lack of awareness of the majority of risk management techniques	People are trained in the process. Awareness of the most commonly used techniques	Different training levels are established. Consistent measures of probability and impact. Expanded risk coverage	Sophisticated robust tools and models in use. Experienced personnel applying judgement to quantified results	Knowledge and skills are updated constantly. Effective use of formal risk management techniques. Risk quantification is fully integrated into business decisions

D11 USE/DEPLOYMENT

Progressing between maturity levels

Once risk maturity within an organisation has been assessed and a model has been constructed, steps can be undertaken to develop specific action plans for improving processes to attain the next level in the model. It is recognised that there are constraints in moving from one level to the next. Although these constraints are not insurmountable they take management time and effort to overcome. For instance to move from a level one to a level two it is common for organisations to address the following issues:

- Develop a risk management process that is tailored to the organisation
- Define the organisation's risk appetite
- Understand, capture and disseminate the anticipated sources of risk
- Develop a risk terminology that will aid embedding risk management in the organisation
- Promulgate the benefits of risk management using examples of completed risk management studies
- Develop straightforward risk management reporting
- Make risk management roles and responsibilities explicit.

Maintaining the highest level of maturity

Once the highest level of maturity has been achieved, effort and resources are required to keep the organisation at that level. It will entail:

- Establishing a continual improvement process
- Using lessons learned to inform and refine existing processes
- Applying audit and review techniques to ensure risk management techniques are as effective as possible in supporting decision-making
- Continuing to invest in improving risk processes, tools, techniques and training to ensure the 'currency' of risk management processes to maintain the organisation's capability
- Keeping policies and internal guidance up-to-date to avoid the risk process becoming outdated and increasingly irrelevant to the organisation and its context
- Applying risk management to all types of activities whether the organisation sees them as projects or not, such as organisational change, outsourcing or entering into new contracts

- Maintaining the risk management culture by including risk management responsibilities into terms of engagement, management processes and key decision-making processes.

Benefits

The growing popularity of maturity models and the breadth of their application stems from the benefits that they can offer organisations. The list below, whilst not exhaustive, describes some of the primary benefits of maturity models.

- They provide organisations with a road map for process improvement that can be readily constructed, assimilated and communicated.
- They provide a vehicle for benchmarking risk management processes.
- They enable organisations to identify what needs to be done in order to improve current processes and increase their ability to manage threats and opportunities.
- They enable organisations to build an action plan of the activities they wish to embark on to improve their processes.
- They afford organisations the opportunity to assess the financial benefits obtained from one level of the model prior to committing resources to implementing the next level.
- When processes are understood and operating at their best, staff are motivated, morale and productivity are high and the quality of outputs is also high. Even the finest people can't perform at their best when working with immature processes.
- They enable the benefits of risk management to be realised in terms of minimising costly project overruns, making informed decisions when selecting between options and making the risk ownership profile of different contracts transparent.
- They support organisations to reach their strategic objectives while at the same time conserving organisational resources.

D12 CONCLUSION

Embarking on the preparation and implementation of a maturity model is likely to involve making a serious commitment of organisational time and resources. It may take some organisations many months and in some instances years to construct and subsequently implement the different maturity levels contained within the model. The development of a maturity model is never intended to provide an immediate fix. This guide does not recommend that organisations that are currently just embarking on introducing risk management practices, attempt to introduce the most mature level of risk management from the outset. This approach is likely to fail.

Developing and embedding effective risk management requires time. Organisations wishing to implement a formal structured approach to risk management need to treat implementation as a project in itself, which requires establishing clear objectives and success criteria and undertaking proper planning, resourcing and effective monitoring and management.

Once completed, a model must be readily understood to be effective and to encourage its adoption, application and ongoing development. The model should be scalable, flexible and adaptable to accommodate changes in an organisation's size, structure, markets or its regulatory context. It must be treated as a live document and be updated when necessary to reflect new standards, guides, techniques or governance regimes.

Where the use of the model can be seen to have directly contributed to process improvement or bottom-line performance, then this success should be shared across the organisation to support embedding the model within ongoing risk management practices.

D13 OTHER EXAMPLES

Included in Table D.3 are examples of level labels included within 10 different publications that are not all specific to risk management. For risk management to continue to be a respected discipline it cannot afford to be purely introspective but must learn from across industry.

Table D.3 Comparison of maturity model levels

Publications	Level 1	Level 2	Level 3	Level 4	Level 5
CCTA[1]	First	Second	Third	Fourth	
Chapman[2]	Initial	Basic	Standard	Advanced	
Hillson[3]	Naive	Novice	Normalised	Natural	
Hopkinson[4]	Naive	Novice	Normalised	Natural	
PRINCE2[5]	Initial	Repeatable	Defined		
OGC P3M3[6]	Initial	Repeatable	Defined	Managed	Optimised
Sun Microsystems[7]	Chaotic	Reactive	Proactive	Optimised	Self-aware
PMI[8]	Standardise	Measure	Control	Continually improve	
FAA[9]	Performed	Managed planned and tracked	Defined	Quantitatively managed	Optimising
RMRP[10]	Ad hoc	Initial	Repeatable	Managed	

1   Government Centre for Information Systems (1993) Introduction to the Management of Risk, October, HMSO, Norwich.
2   Chapman, R.J. (2006) Simple tools and techniques for enterprise management of risk, John Wiley and Sons Ltd., England.
3   Hillson, D (1997) Towards a Risk Maturity Model, International Journal of Project & Business Management of risk, Volume 1, Issue 1, pages 35-45, January.
4   Hopkinson, M. (2000) Risk Maturity Models in Practice, Management of risk Bulletin, Vol 5, Issue 4
5   OGC (2004) PRINCE2 Maturity Model V0.05.01.
6   Office of Government Commerce (2006) Portfolio, programme & project management maturity model (p3m3) 1st February, Version 1.0.
7   Sun Microsystems, (2005) Information lifecycle management maturity model white paper, April.
8   Organizational Project Management Maturity Model (OPM3®) Project Management Institute (PMI), PMI Global Operations Center, Newtown Square, Pennsylvania US.
9   Federal Aviation Administration FAA-integrated Capability Maturity Model (FAA-iCMM).
10 RMRP (2002) Management of risk Maturity Level Development, Management of risk Research and Development Program Collaboration (INCOSE/PMI/APM).

Risk specialisms

Appendix E: Risk specialisms

The purpose of this appendix is to provide introductions to some risk specialisms and direct the reader to more detailed information on these specialisms. The specialisms covered are:

- Business continuity management
- Incident (crisis) management
- Health and safety
- Security
- Financial risk management.

E1 BUSINESS CONTINUITY MANAGEMENT IN A RISK CONTEXT

Business continuity management (BCM) complements the wider risk management programme. Risk management is an integral part of BCM and helps to manage risk around the critical activities that enable an organisation to continue operating following an event or incident. BCM incorporates risk identification, assessment and control in relation to the activities, products and services on which the organisation depends, and which need to be operational in time to enable the organisation to retain credibility and continue to meet its responsibilities.

Through BCM, an organisation can identify and plan what needs to be done before an incident occurs to ensure its people, reputation, assets, systems and information remain secure and operational.

With that recognition, the organisation can then take a risk informed view on the responses that may be needed when disruption occurs, so that it can be confident that it will manage its risks through any consequences without unacceptable delay in delivering its products or services.

> *Progressive organisations now regard BCM not as a costly planning process, but as a key value added improvement process firmly integrated with risk management. BS25999-1:2006*

Figure E.1 BCM lifecycle (BSI BS25999-1DPC)

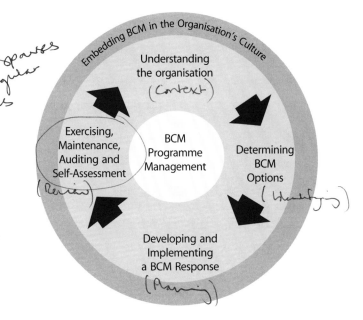

The individual steps within the lifecycle can be explained as follows:

BCM programme management

Programme management enables the business continuity capability to be established (if necessary) and maintained in a manner appropriate to the size and complexity of the organisation.

Understanding the organisation

The activities associated with the 'Understanding the organisation' stage provide information that enables prioritisation of an organisation's products and services and the urgency of the activities that are required to deliver them. This sets the requirements that will determine the selection of appropriate BCM strategies.

As part of the 'Understanding the organisation' stage within the business continuity lifecycle, the organisation should identify and evaluate specific threats and vulnerabilities to its critical activities along with ways in which they could potentially disrupt these activities.

In particular the organisation should consider:

- Internal threats, such as fire, accidental damage, failures (of IT systems, LAN, WAN, voice systems, and telecommunications), staff shortage/loss, theft of critical equipment/documents, human error, wilful damage and viruses
- External threats, such as flooding, natural disasters, terrorist or extremist group activity, loss of dependent facilities/suppliers, strikes and nearby hazard sites.

Using the identified threats, the organisation should identify mitigating/risk reduction actions to ensure it can continue its critical activities and thereby continue to meet its responsibilities.

The purpose of the risk assessment is to identify measures that would:

- Reduce the likelihood of a disruptive event
- Shorten the period of disruption
- Limit the impact on the organisation's critical activities.

As part of this BCM risk identification, assessment, and control activity, organisations and the business continuity manager would be expected to refer to and use the Risk Registers held within the organisation as a starting point and would be expected to add to these registers as they encounter additional business risks during the BCM process.

Determining business continuity strategies

Determining business continuity strategies enables a range of strategies to be evaluated. This allows an appropriate response to be chosen for each product or service, such that the organisation can continue to deliver those products and services:

- At an acceptable level of operation
- Within an acceptable timeframe during and following a disruption.

The choice made will take account of the resilience and countermeasure options already present within the organisation.

Developing and implementing a BCM response

Developing and implementing a BCM response results in the creation of a management framework and a structure of incident management, business continuity and business recovery plans that detail the steps to be taken during and after an incident to maintain or restore operations.

BCM exercising, maintaining and reviewing BCM arrangements

BCM exercising, maintenance, review and audit lead to the organisation being able to:

- Demonstrate the extent to which its strategies and plans are complete, current and accurate
- Identify opportunities for improvement
- Assess ongoing BCM capability and maturity.

Embedding BCM in the organisation's culture

Embedding BCM in the organisation's culture enables BCM to become part of the organisation's core values and instils confidence in all stakeholders in the ability of the organisation to cope with disruptions. This step in the BCM lifecycle includes the education, training and awareness activities to promote and maintain an understanding of BCM, the organisation's response and the responsibilities that each individual has.

Further information

Further information on BCM processes, good practice and industry information can be obtained from one or more of the following:

- BS 25999-1:2006 (available from the British Standards Institute, www.BSI-global.com)
- Business Continuity Institute Good Practice Guide (available from the Business Continuity Institute, www.thebci.org.uk)
- Disaster Recovery Institute International Professional Practices for Business Continuity Professionals (www.drii.org)

E2 INCIDENT (CRISIS) MANAGEMENT

Incident management is an integral part of business continuity. It is the process by which an organisation manages the wider impact of an incident until it is either under control or contained without impact to the organisation or until the business continuity plan is invoked.

In the same way that emergency response time is critical, so is the response time to a potential or actual crisis. A 'golden hour' exists after the identification of a crisis; this is when the type and nature of response is crucial, a professional, structured and well thought-out response to a crisis has the ability to turn a potentially disastrous incident into an opportunity and enable the risks and impacts to the business to be contained. If a crisis is managed inefficiently or is perceived to be badly handled, this can have a devastating effect on the organisation and its stakeholders, escalating the crisis to higher proportions.

One of the aims of detailed and well-constructed business continuity management is to include an incident management plan and response within the development programme, thereby building incident management capability to avoid incidents developing into a crisis. An incident management plan is described as 'a coordinated organisation-wide response to the incident, including communication with the stakeholders, such as staff, customers, shareholders and the media' (BS25999-1:2006).

The purpose of the incident management plan is to enable the organisation to manage the immediate stages of an incident. This should address the stakeholder and external issues facing the organisation during an incident. It is vital that the incident management plan is also flexible, feasible/practical, relevant, and easy to read, understand and follow. It should provide the basis for managing and coordinating most possible issues arising from a threat to the business. The threats should be identified as part of the risk assessment activity early in the business continuity process. The primary aims of the incident management plan are to:

- Ensure the safety of all affected individuals
- Contain the incident to minimise further loss.

In the same way that business continuity requires support, so does the incident management plan, and it is vital that it:

- Has board-level support, including a sponsor and nominated owner
- Is supported by an appropriate budget for development, maintenance and training.

BS25999-1:2006 provides further details and guidance on developing incident management plans and responses.

E3   HEALTH AND SAFETY

It is good management practice to protect your investment. The most important asset of an organisation is its people, and ensuring their safety is a major responsibility and a legal obligation. Health and safety legislation relates to all aspects of people within a working environment. This is a specialist area and requires adequate training as well as fully assigned responsibility for ensuring adequate controls are in place.

In the area of health, safety and welfare there are various regulations and sets of legislation. These include:

- Workplace (Health and Safety and Welfare) Regulations

- Buildings-related regulations (for example, Electricity at Work Regulations covering ergonomics, lighting, noise levels and air quality, for example)
- Fire Precautions
- Control of Hazardous Substances
- Working Time Regulations (based on EU Working Time Directive)
- EU Part-Time Working Directive.
- The Health and Safety Executive produces much guidance in this area, including links to expert guidance, risk assessment steps and specific guidance and information on health and safety, the law and management.

For further information consult the Health and Safety Executive's website at www.hse.gov.uk

E4   SECURITY

Risk management within the 'Security' sphere incorporates physical and logical security (i.e. physical, information, personnel and technical). Security is about maintaining the confidentiality, availability and integrity of an asset; therefore security risk management looks at, assesses and develops an appropriate approach or treatment for risks relating to the security of those assets. The threats are those activities that could affect the confidentiality, integrity or availability of the asset.

The same risk management principles, techniques and process should be applied to security risks as are applied to any other risks.

There is an increasing amount of legislation relevant to security, either in terms of compliance that is required, or how information is collected, stored, used/processed and provided to legal bodies, for example:

- Data Protection Act (DPA)
- Electronic Communications Act
- Public Records Act
- Regulation of Investigatory Powers Act
- The Lawful Business Practice Regulations
- Computer Misuse Act
- European Software directive
- Copyright, design and patents Act
- The Official Secrets Act
- Telecommunication Act
- Broadcasting Act
- Anti-Terrorism, Crime and Security Act
- Human Rights Act
- Police and Criminal Evidence Act

- Civil Evidence Act
- Criminal Justice Act
- Civil Contingencies Act
- Freedom of Information Act.

The British Standards Institute documents on Information Security Management and on Security Management should be reviewed and consulted to ensure that good practice is being adopted.

Everyone within an organisation has a responsibility for security in some form. People need to understand this responsibility, and the level of accountability and the procedures that apply to them. The main areas that need to be considered for security purposes are:

- Information
- Personnel
- Physical
- Technical.

There are overlaps between some of these categories – in particular, technical and document security. These overlaps may sometimes be difficult to clarify. BS7799/ISO 27001 applies to the area of information security management, other key areas to consider are outlined below.

Personnel security

Organisations will wish to make arrangements to check staff and consultants that are to work for them. There may be different levels of clearance required for security purposes. The levels and circumstances to which they apply should be clearly documented. The required security check should be undertaken as part of the recruitment process. In many cases this will simply involve taking up a number of references. These references may relate to personal or business associations. Additionally, when a person's role within the organisation changes, a change of clearance level may be required.

Physical security

Access to buildings: this should cover ensuring access at a business location, and it should take account of the impact of fire, flood and terrorism, and risks to transport infrastructure. It should also ensure that only authorised people gain access to the building or parts of the building. Arrangements should cover staff, consultants and other visitors.

Access to information: only those people with appropriate authority are allowed access to the organisation's information. An important consideration is the Data Protection Act, which requires suitable controls for the handling of personal information.

Availability of resources: people or equipment must be available at the right time and place to fulfil the business requirement. This should take account of the facilities people need, and whether the building is adequately heated, supplied with water, sewerage systems and so on.

Technical security

This aspect needs to consider the security requirements of technology-related assets, in particular IT networks, systems and equipment. This has to be balanced with enabling staff to make appropriate use of equipment so that they can perform their designated business function. Topics that require specific consideration for IT equipment include:

- Use of internal networks
- Internet access
- Email
- Viruses
- Hacking
- Remote working
- Backing up information (particularly from laptops).

Relevant British and international standards for security management include:

- BS 7799-1:2005 (ISO 17799:2005) Information Technology – Security Techniques – Code of Practice for Information Security Management
- BS 7799-2:2005 (ISO 27001:2005) Information Technology – Security Techniques – Information Security Management Systems – Requirements
- BS 7799-3:2006 Information Security Management Systems – Guidelines for Information Security Risk Management

E5   FINANCIAL RISK MANAGEMENT

Financial risk management is the practice by which an organisation optimises the manner in which it takes financial risk. This includes the monitoring of financial risk taking activities, upholding relevant financial and operational policies and procedures through appropriate controls, and the production and distribution of financial risk-related reports.

Financial risk management does not mean simply optimising risk. That is the province of the board of directors and senior management, working with more tactical risk takers such as investment companies/advisers, financial directors/Accounting Officers, traders or portfolio managers. Financial risk management is about optimising the manner in which financial risks are assessed and taken.

Accordingly, financial risk management isn't about managing anything. It is really about facilitating.

Functionally, there are four aspects of financial risk management and on which success depends. These are all closely related and akin to principles for overall good risk management practice but have been specifically publicised for financial risk management following a number of financial risk management failures (such as Enron and Barings). The four aspects of financial risk management are:

- A positive corporate culture
- Actively observed policies and procedures
- Effective use of technology
- Independence of risk management professionals.

Culture

While individual initiative is critical, it is corporate culture that facilitates the process. Corporate culture defines what behaviour the members of an organisation will condone – and what behaviour they will shun. Corporate culture plays a critical role in financial risk management because it defines the risks that an individual must personally take if he or she is going to help manage organisational risks.

A positive risk culture is one that promotes individual responsibility and is supportive of risk taking. Characteristics include:

- **Individuals making decisions:** Group decision-making can be ineffective if no one is personally accountable. When a single person makes a decision – possibly with the help or approval of others – that individual is accountable. His or her reputation is on the line, so he or she will carefully analyse the issues before proposing a course of action.
- **Questioning:** In a positive risk culture, people question everything. Not only does this identify better ways to do things, but it also ensures that people understand and appreciate procedures.
- **Admissions of ignorance:** Admitting that we don't know entails significant personal risk. A positive risk culture supports such honesty at every level of an organisation.

Policies and procedures

The purpose of policies and procedures is to empower people. They specify how people can accomplish what needs to be done. It is only when policies and procedures are neglected or abused that they become an impediment.

The success of policies and procedures depends critically on a positive risk culture. Hundreds of pages of procedures, neatly printed and sitting on a shelf, are useless if no one uses them. Even a simple set of procedures, however, can make an enormous difference for an organisation if people believe in them and take personal responsibility for upholding them.

Examples of procedures include:

- **Board procedures:** Every board of directors or governing body should operate under a set of procedures that address conflicts of interest, clarify personal responsibility and facilitate the discussion and resolution of difficult or contentious issues.
- **Lines of reporting:** Everyone in an organisation should report to a single person. The line of reporting should be explicit. A worthwhile illustration for this is the Bank of England's report on the Barings' collapse. That report identifies four different people who may have had oversight responsibility for Nick Leeson.
- **Trading authority:** Whenever an organisation engages in a new form of market activity – such as the use of a new form of transaction, a new investment strategy or proprietary trading – there should first be a formal review and approval process. A streamlined procedure should apply for granting new responsibility.
- **Risk limits:** Market and credit risk limits represent procedures for managing financial risk. There should also be procedures for establishing and reviewing such limits in order to assure that the system of limits remains effective.

Technology

The primary role technology plays in financial risk management is risk assessment and communication. Technology is employed to quantify or otherwise summarise risks as they are being taken. It then communicates this information to decision-makers, as appropriate. Technology might include a Value at Risk (VaR) system or portfolio credit risk system. It can include financial engineering technology for independently marking to market positions. It may include an interactive risk report that is electronically circulated to managers every day.

For many institutions, such as banks or securities firms, technology is a critical component of financial risk management. For other organisations, including some non-financial corporations or pension plans, technology plays a lesser role.

Independence

For financial risk management to succeed, risk managers must be independent of risk taking functions within the organisation. Independence can be defined as comprising the following four criteria:

- Risk managers have reporting lines that are independent from those of risk taking functions.
- Except at the highest levels, risk takers have no input on the performance reviews, compensation or promotion of risk managers, and vice versa.
- Employees cannot undertake a position within the organisation that allows them to fulfil both roles. Those hired into financial risk management undertake the role of financial risk management; those hired as risk takers undertake the role of risk takers.
- Risk managers are not employed to take risks on the firm's behalf, they are employed to help identify risks and quantify/qualify those risks. They do not necessarily advise on which risks to take. They express no opinions about the desirability of any particular risks.

It is important to distinguish between risk taking and risk management. Within firms, there are strategic and tactical risk takers. The CEO and other senior managers are strategic risk takers. They formulate a strategy for the firm that entails taking certain risks. They communicate the strategy to tactical risk takers – including traders, structures and asset managers – whose job it is to implement that strategy.

Financial risk managers fit into one of two competing models.

- According to one model, they identify risks that should be avoided and, in doing so, risks that should be taken. In this manner, risk managers help the less qualified strategic and tactical risk takers do their jobs.
- The alternative model is that they act as facilitators. Strategic and tactical risk takers are responsible for deciding what risks to take. Financial risk managers facilitate the process by ensuring effective communication between the two groups. They help strategic risk takers communicate through policies, procedures and risk limits. They help tactical risk takers communicate by preparing risk reports that describe the risks they are taking.

Further sources of useful information on financial risk management are:

- Basel Committee: *International Convergence of Capital Measurement and Capital Standards: a Revised Framework* (text of the Basel II Accord)
- Global Association of Risk Professionals (www.garp.com)
- The Committee of Sponsoring Organisations of the Treadway Agreement (COSO) on which most financial controls are based (www.coso.org/publications.htm)

Selecting risk management software tools

F

Appendix F: Selecting risk management software tools

F1   INTRODUCTION

Suitable software support tools are essential for the efficient implementation of risk management. Software tools range from spreadsheets and databases to sophisticated modelling tools. This appendix aims to provide managers with an indication of the things to consider when planning the selection of a tool to assist in the implementation of risk management.

Appendix B looks at techniques as inputs to the risk management process. Many of these techniques can be supported by tools. Some tools will have a broad application; others will have a more specific use.

It is recommended that when considering the acquisition of a support tool, it is best managed as a project. The project should establish the need for the tool, justify its acquisition and make sure that the right resources are available to install it and that implementation is supported by training.

The following guidance provides general advice on tool selection rather than being specific to risk management tools. Many of these tools support a wide range of activities, and all aspects, not just specific risk management ones, need to form part of the assessment.

Software tools support all of the steps in the management of risk process including stakeholder analysis diagrams, schedule analysis, risk breakdown structures, cause and effect diagrams, Risk Registers, database construction, Monte Carlo and Latin hypercube analysis, graphs, cost models, investment modelling and word processing.

F2   ISSUES TO CONSIDER WHEN SELECTING TOOLS

There are a number of issues to consider when selecting and adopting a tool for use within the organisation. These include:

- Having a well-defined need in terms of what improvements can be made to manual processes
- Developing the identified need into a fully developed business case that clearly articulates the objectives, benefits, costs, timeframe, organisational interfaces and assumptions

- Recognising that if the business case is accepted then the requirements of the software package need to be captured
- Establishing weighting criteria. As each requirement will not be of equal importance, it will be important to ensure that when assessing alternative products those products that meet the key requirements score higher than those that satisfy ancillary requirements
- Identifying suitable products for consideration
- Short-listing products that meet the requirements to varying degrees
- Scoring the products using both a scoring system and the weighting criteria
- Making the final selection based on a series of issues including the scoring, the cost, contract terms, licences, support, adaptability of the product and the training required.

To make an objective judgement it is useful to take a structured approach to the review of products and their capabilities. This will provide the information required to make the subsequent selection while meeting procurement and organisational requirements.

F3   GENERIC SELECTION PROCESS

The overall objective of the selection process (once the need has been justified through the development of a satisfactory business case), is to identify the best match from among all of the off-the-shelf proprietary software products that might meet a requirement. The process incrementally reduces the number of candidate products through several stages until the final choice. This process has grown in importance due to the proliferation of risk software products now available.

Figure F.1 below describes the simple steps in a generic process for the selection of a product, which will require tailoring to suit the particular needs of an organisation. It is possible that not all of these activities will be performed in every situation, or adopted to the same level of detail.

Figure F.1 Generic proprietary software selection process

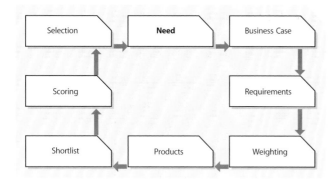

F4 DEFINITION OF NEED

There must be a clear understanding of the need in terms of what the organisation wishes to accomplish, how it believes it is currently constrained or how it understands it can improve its current processes. Time should be taken to make the need as explicit as possible as this will support both the preparation of a business case and a requirements schedule. If it is thought for instance that a database is required, consider the deficiencies of the current processes, how these processes can be improved, how the quality of the information is affected, whether the database offers savings in time, whether it improves or reduces reliability, and how recipients of the outputs would register any differences.

F5 BUSINESS CASE

The business case documents information necessary to support any decision to invest in software tools. Concise, well-written business cases help organisations: make the right investment decisions; achieve whole-life value for money from investments; enable changes to proposals; and realise the benefits of those investments. The business case must provide a clear understanding of what needs to be done, why it needs to be done now, why there is no better way to achieve this objective and why this is a wise use of resources.

Making the right investment decision depends on ensuring that from a strategic perspective, the investment results in (or at least contributes to) either the achievement of both high-level strategic and subordinate objectives, at the right time, in the right sequence or coordination with other investments.

To make a judgement as to whether the investment is the right one in strategic terms, it is necessary to have a clear understanding of the contribution that the investment will make to the achievement of strategic objectives and

development plans (relative to those of other investments that could be made). Such a judgement relies on:

- Assurance that the intended benefits are indeed realistic and realisable
- A clear understanding of the sequence in which the benefits would be realisable as a result of the investment
- The contribution of the intended benefits to the achievement of policy outcomes or strategic objectives
- Strategic fit within the context of any wider inter-organisational programmes
- Strategic fit within the context of the organisation's current services and services in development
- Breakdown of anticipated expenditure and hence a justification of the amount of required budget
- Economic payback (when assessed financially and measured using NPV, ROI or ROCE).

To achieve consensus as to what benefits are realistically achievable as a result of a change, it will be necessary to involve stakeholders, possibly through one or more workshops.

F6 REQUIREMENTS

It is important to prepare a requirements schedule to enable a comparative analysis of alternative vendor products to be undertaken in a systematic, consistent and reliable manner. The requirements need to be carefully considered to avoid the wrong choice being made. An inappropriate product can slow down the production of robust information that decision-makers rely on, rather than improve processes. Organisations find it helpful to subdivide their requirements into high-level 'must haves' and ancillary supporting functionality.

High-level view of criteria for software tools

The top-level criteria are:

- Functionality – the knowledge representation techniques and inference methods provided
- Developer interface – the facilities available to the developer, and the skills required for application development using the product
- Integration – the degree to which the product integrates with other software
- Efficiency – development and run-time machine resource usage
- Development methodology – the degree to which the tool supports any of the emerging methodologies for developing knowledge-based systems

- Quality and control – the facilities available for, and the degree to which it is possible to ensure, high-quality software engineering
- Portability – the range of hardware platforms and operating systems on which the product will run, and the extent to which the development environment or individual applications are transferable
- End-user interface – the facilities available for developing end-user interfaces
- Security – protection and control of access to data and knowledge, and to the tool itself, especially the development environment
- Workgroup support – the ability for multiple employees to collaborate on a common project with configurable levels of access to data
- Product credibility – status of the product and supplier, and degree of support, release strategy and training
- Project-specific criteria – other than the above.

Low-level view of criteria for software tools:

- Requirements – is there a requirement for a particular operating or database system or other prerequisite software that could conflict with the IT department's standard end-user software environment?
- Data transfer – is it important to export or import data in the application. For example, is there a requirement to export data to Microsoft Office applications for statistical purposes if the application is weak on reports? Is there a requirement to interface some of the outputs with other software packages or to migrate data from other risk management software already in use?
- Finding data – for database software, when searching for data on the system is it easy to use? Are there several ways of finding the data that the users will need? How easy is it to find specific data such as a particular record? Also, how easy is it gain access to the documents and reference information that may be stored in the system?
- Flexibility – are there sufficient look-up tables or drop-down lists that offer a selection of data to choose from when using the system? Are they user configurable?
- Links – will it handle links and hyperlinks to external records and information? For example, is there a need for it to be able to link to documents or data within other external systems?
- Users – does the software support the required number of users (and concurrent users), have the required archive capabilities and support any remote working requirements?

- Sites – is multi-site operation required or is support required on a single site?
- Relationships – does the database system display a graphical representation of a hierarchical structure (parent/child relationships)?
- Compliance – does it comply with statutory standards such as ISO9000?
- Implementation – how much work is required to implement the software? Is it simply a case of installing it on a server on your network and mapping drives to it? Does it require a lot of expensive, on-site consultancy?
- Maintenance – what are the levels of maintenance required? For example, are manual database backup and archiving processes required?
- Location – is there a requirement for users to log on and input or check data from any workstation that has the application installed and can this be achieved by remote users who may not have a permanent connection to the organisation's corporate network? Is this important?
- Login – can login be achieved quickly and effortlessly?
- Access speed – does the software conform to requirements with regard to speed of access and response time?
- Customisation – is it possible to customise screens for example to allow the administrator to hide specific fields from defined users?
- Proficiency – is the software suitable for the level of proficiency of your intended users?
- Reports – how readily can reports be accessed and found on the system. Can the reports be customised? Can data be exported to Excel?

Customisation of criteria

Although generic checklists of criteria for assessment are helpful, they should always be made task or project specific. They should be customised. This customisation compromises the following steps:

- Alter criteria – the criteria may need to be altered in places to meet specific requirements
- Add criteria – some projects, especially those that are not standard administrative systems, may have special requirements that need incorporation into the list of evaluation criteria
- Omit criteria – some of the criteria may be irrelevant to a particular project and may be omitted
- Combine criteria – it may be necessary to use all of the detail and criteria together and to combine evaluation hierarchies

- Prioritise criteria – once criteria have been added, omitted or modified it may be appropriate to re-evaluate the priority of the criteria to ensure the correct assessment is made
- Annotate the criteria – it is often desirable, particularly if a team is undertaking the evaluation, to annotate the criteria with specific guidelines on evaluation and scoring.

Evaluation teams should guard against the following when carrying out customisation:

- Oversimplification – if too few criteria are used then insufficient detail may be gathered and it may not be possible to evaluate the products adequately
- Appropriateness – the criteria are designed to be generic, so their applicability to the project must be defined in each case
- Extensive alteration – the criteria and hierarchies suggested are based on long experience and should meet most requirements. Although it is necessary for them to be tailored to reflect the requirements, extensive divergence should be approached with caution.

F7   WEIGHTING

As the requirements do not all have the same degree of importance (in terms of their contribution to the overall usefulness of the product), it is helpful to apply a weighting to each requirement. The weighting is a measure of the relative importance of each requirement. The justification for the allocation of the weights should be recorded. It is suggested that a weighting factor of between 0-4 is selected for each feature or requirement. This should reflect the importance of the feature.

Typical weighting factor definitions are shown in Table F.1:

F8   PRODUCTS

Product identification is the process of drawing up a list of candidate products. How diligently this step is conducted will directly influence the degree of choice that is available. Assistance on finding suitable products can be obtained from professional institutes, the web, and specialist publications.

F9   SHORT-LISTING

The objective of this initial short-listing process is to reduce the list of candidate products to a number that can reasonably be assessed (each of which should be capable of satisfying the essential requirements) without having to resort to detailed technical product evaluation. This whole procedure is one of reducing the list of products on the market to a shortlist of those that best meet the organisation's requirements. Attending demonstrations is usually only useful for experienced staff who are familiar with a range of products, and are able to put what they see into context and ask the relevant questions.

F10 SCORING

The short-listed products are now looked at in greater detail with the aim of allocating a score to each requirement. The assigned scores should be backed up by a set of working notes summarising the considerations that resulted in the scores given. Apart from providing justification for the comparative markings, the notes will prove invaluable if it becomes necessary to review the scoring at a later stage (e.g. because of the introduction of a new version of a product).

The score should reflect how well the application handles each feature.

Table F.1 Typical weighting factor definitions

0 Not important	(Select 0 or ignore if the feature is not a requirement)
1 Has some significance	(Select 1 if the feature would have limited benefit)
2 Significant	(Select 2 if the feature is one that you prefer to have but on which you could possibly compromise)
3 Highly significant	(Select 3 if the feature is one that you would not like to be without)
4 Absolute or mandatory requirement	(Select 4 if the feature is an absolute necessity for which there is no compromise)

The following scoring system is commonly adopted:

4. Fully meets requirement
3. Partially meets requirement
2. Can be modified or developed or will accommodate a work around.
1. Available in next revision
0. Does not meet requirement

Then the weight is multiplied by the score to give the weighted score.

The process is performed for each product in turn, providing at the end of the evaluation an aggregate score for each product. The list of comparative scores gives the ranking of the products in terms of how well they meet the technical requirements of the evaluation.

F11 SELECTING

Selection will be dependent on a combination of issues including the scoring completed in the previous step, the costs, training requirements, the licensing structure, planned product development, product support and limitations.

Cost

- Cost of software – assess the application for bottom-line cost for the configuration and number of users that you require.
- Cost of hardware – what is the bottom-line cost of any additional hardware required to making the product active?
- Potential future cost – what is the likelihood of significant future costs?
- Implementation cost – implementation costs may include items such as installation of the software and consultancy. You should consider this for each application.
- Training cost – what are the training costs involved in implementing this application?
- Cost of customisation – are there any costs involved in customising the product for your requirements.
- Licences – are licences required for additional database software such as SQL server?

Vendor profile

- Stability – each vendor's stability must be assessed. How long have they been in business? How long have they been selling this type of software? When was this application first developed? How many local and international clients do they have for the application?
- Professionalism – assess each vendor for the professionalism displayed in dealing with your inquiry and in demonstrating their products.
- Service level agreement – assess each vendor for the level of future service and support that they offer. Do they provide telephone support at the times you require it? Do they provide online help? What does it cost for the level of service that you require?
- Provision of customisation – can the application be customised and what are the costs involved?
- Upgrade path – if the application is an entry-level system that you may upgrade in future, assess the vendor for the upgrade path offered and the cost of these upgrades.
- Customer base – how many packages has the vendor sold and who buys them?
- Support for add-ons – some software packages use add-ons to make them more comprehensive. If the use of add-ons or third-party modules is important, evaluate the software for this.

Further information

Further information

All dates are correct at the time of publication.

GUIDANCE ON CORPORATE GOVERNANCE AND INTERNAL CONTROL

- Cadbury Committee on the Financial Aspects of Corporate Governance (1992) *Report of the Committee on the Financial Aspects of Corporate Governance: The Code of Best Practice*, Gee Publishing.
- Greenbury Study Group (1995) *Report on Directors' Remuneration*, Gee Publishing.
- Hampel Committee on Corporate Governance (1998) *Committee on Corporate Governance: Final Report*, Gee Publishing.
- Institute of Chartered Accountants of England and Wales – ICAEW (1999) *Internal Control: Guidance for Directors on the Combined Code*, published by the Internal Control Working Party of the Institute of Chartered Accountants in England and Wales led by Nigel Turnbull, September 1999.
- Institute of Chartered Accountants in England and Wales – ICAEW (September 1999) *Implementing Turnbull, A Boardroom Briefing, Centre for Business Performance*, Jones, E. M. and Sutherland, G.
- CIPFA and SOLACE (2001) *Corporate Governance in Local Government – A Keystone for Community Governance: The Framework*, published by CIPFA, The Chartered Institute of Public Finance and Accountancy, London.
- CIPFA (2003) *Guidance on Internal Control and Risk Management in Principal Local Authorities and other Relevant Bodies to Support Compliance with the Accounts and Audit Regulations 2003*, published by CIPFA, The Chartered Institute of Public Finance and Accountancy, London.
- Higgs Review (2003) *Review of the Role and Effectiveness of Non-Executive Directors*, published by the Department of Trade and Industry, UK. Printed by TSO (The Stationery Office).
- *The Tyson Report on the Recruitment and Development of Non-Executive Directors* (2003), London Business School (www.london.edu).
- *The Listing Rules* (2003), Financial Services Agency, London.
- Combined Code on Corporate Governance (June 2003), Financial Reporting Council, CCH.

- Financial Reporting Council (2003) *Audit Committees Combined Code Guidance*. A report and proposed guidance by an FRC appointed group chaired by Sir Robert Smith (2003), The Financial Reporting Council Limited (FRC), January.
- Financial Reporting Council (2005) Internal Control – Revised Guidance for Directors on the Combined Code.
- Sheridan, F., *Implementing Sarbanes-Oxley Section 404*, forming Section 3.3 of *Managing Business Risk, a Practical Guide to Protecting your Business* (2003), consultant editor Jolly, A., published by Kogan Page Limited, Great Britain and US, p81-89.
- OECD (2004) *OECD Principles of Corporate Governance*, OECD Publications Service, France.
- COSO (2004) *Enterprise Risk Management – Integrated Framework*, September, published by The Committee of Sponsoring Organisations of the Treadway Commission.
- Toronto Stock Exchange Committee on Corporate Governance in Canada (1994) *Where Were The Directors?* TSE, Canada, December.

GUIDANCE ON RISK MANAGEMENT

- Cabinet Office (2000) *Successful IT: Modernising Government in Action*, Cabinet Office, HM Government, London, May.
- National Audit Office (2000) *Supporting Innovation: Managing Risk in Government Departments*. Report by the Comptroller and Auditor General, 17 August, London, TSO.
- BSI PD 6668 (2000) *Managing Risk for Corporate Governance*, 2001 reprint, British Standards Institute, London, UK.
- Audit Commission (2001) *Worth the Risk?*
- Cabinet Office (2002) *Risk improving government's capability to handle risk and uncertainty*, Strategy Unit, Cabinet Office, HM Government, London.
- Institute of Risk Management (2002) A Risk Management Standard.
- HM Treasury (2003) *Appraisal and Evaluation in Central Government*, HM Treasury, published by TSO (the *Green Book*). First edition 1991, second edition 1997.
- HM Treasury (2004) *Management of Risk – Principles and Concepts* (the *Orange Book*) revised.

- HM Treasury (2004) *Managing Risks with Delivery Partners*.
- NAO (2004) *Managing Risks to Improve Public Sector*.
- CIPFA (2004) *The Risk Management Journey – A self-assessment and Audit Check*.
- HM Treasury (2006) *Risk: Good Practice in Government* Volumes 1 and 2, HMSO.
- HM Treasury (2006) *Thinking about your Risk: Setting and Communicating your Risk Appetite*, HMSO.
- HM Treasury (2006) *Managing your Risk Appetite: A Practitioner's Guide*, HMSO.
- HM Treasury (2006) *Thinking about Risk: Managing your Risk Appetite: Good Practice Examples*, HMSO.

GUIDANCE ON RISK SPECIALISMS

Business continuity management

- BS 25999-1:2006 (available from the British Standards Institute www.BSI-global.com).
- Business Continuity Institute Good Practice Guide (available from the Business Continuity Institute www.thebci.org.uk).
- Disaster Recovery Institute International Professional practices for Business Continuity professionals (www.drii.org).

Health and safety

- Workplace (Health and Safety and Welfare) Regulations 1992.
- Buildings-related regulations (for example, Electricity at Work Regulations [1989] covering, among other things, ergonomics, lighting, noise levels and air quality).
- Fire Precautions (1997).
- Control of Hazardous Substances (1998).
- Working Time Regulations (1998) (based on EU Working Time Directive).
- EU Part-Time Working Directive (2000).
- The Health and Safety Executive produces much guidance in this area, including links to expert guidance, risk assessment steps and specific guidance and information on health and safety, the law and management.

Security management

- BS 7799-1:2005 (ISO 17799:2005) Information Technology – Security Techniques – Code of Practice for Information Security Management.

- BS 7799-2:2005 (ISO 27001:2005) Information Technology – Security Techniques – Information Security Management Systems – Requirements.
- BS 7799-3:2006 Information Security Management Systems – Guidelines for Information Security Risk Management.

Financial risk management

- Basel Committee (2004). *International Convergence of Capital Measurement and Capital Standards: a Revised Framework* (text of the Basel II Accord).
- Global Association of Risk Professionals (www.garp.com).
- The Committee of Sponsoring Organisations of the Treadway Agreement (COSO) on which most financial controls are based (www.coso.org/publications/htm).

REPORTS AND RESEARCH

- Reports to PM about the Risk Programme: www.hm-treasury.gsi.gov.uk/gfm/RST/ReporttoPM.htm
- Risk Programme – Steering Group papers: www.hm-treasury.gsi.gov.uk/GFM/RST/SteeringGroup.htm
- Strategy Unit report on risk management: www.number-10.gov.uk/SU/RISK/risk/home.html
- Innovation in the Public Sector: www.strategy.gov.uk/files/pdf/pubinov1.pdf
- UK Parliamentary Accounts Committee Report on IT Projects: www.publications.parliament.uk/pa/cm/cmpubacc.htm
- UK Cabinet Office, European Centre for Business Excellence (2006) Innovation and Risk Management: A Recipe for Performance Improvement
- UK OGC/NAO (2004) Common Causes of Project Failure

OTHER REFERENCES

- Association for Project Management (2007) *Project Risk Analysis and Management Guide*, APM
- Chapman, R. J. (1998) The effectiveness of working group risk identification and assessment techniques, *International Journal of Project Management*, Vol. 16, No 6, pp 333-343.
- Chapman, Robert, J. (2006) Simple Tools and Techniques for Enterprise Risk Management, John Wiley and Sons Limited, England.
- Chapman, Robert, J. (2002) *Retaining Design Team Members, a Risk Management Approach*, RIBA Enterprises, England.

- Cooper, B. (2004) *The ICSA Handbook of Good Boardroom Practice*, ICSA Publishing Limited, London.
- Day, A.L. (2001) *Mastering Financial Modelling, a Practitioner's Guide to Applied Corporate Finance*, Pearson Education Limited, London, UK.
- Holliwell, J. (1998) *The Financial Risk Manual, a Systematic Guide to Identifying and Managing Financial Risk*, Pearson Education Limited, London, UK.
- Knight, R. F. and Petty, D. J. (2001) *Philosophies of Risk, Shareholder Value and the CEO, within Mastering Risk Volume 1: Concepts*, editor James Pickford, Pearson Education Limited, London, UK.
- Lam, J. (2003) *Enterprise Risk Management, from Incentives to Controls*, John Wiley & Sons Inc., New Jersey, US.

Glossary

Glossary

ACRONYMS LIST

BCM	Business continuity management
BCP	Business continuity plan
BCPG	Business Continuity Planning Guide produced by UK government property advisers (now part of OGC)
BIA	Business Impact Analysis
BIR (BCPG)	Business Impact Review
BSI	British Standards Institution
CCTA	Central Computer and Telecommunications Agency, one of the organisations that was merged to form OGC
CEO	Chief Executive Officer
COTS	Commercial Off The Shelf
CPA	Critical path analysis
CPM	Critical path method
CRAMM	A risk analysis and management method developed by the UK government to protect IT systems/services
HAZOP	A risk assessment method standing for 'hazard and operability analysis, Risk Registers and databases'
HSE	Health and Safety Executive
IC (BCPG)	Incident Control
ICAEW	Institute of Chartered Accountants of England and Wales
ILGRA	Interdepartmental Liaison Group for Risk Assessment, secretariat provided by HSE
IRR	Internal Rate of Return
IS	Information System
IT	Information Technology
ITIL®	The OGC IT Infrastructure Library, a set of guides on the management and provision of operational IT services
LCC	Lifecycle Costings
M_o_R®	Management of Risk (the brand name for this guidance)

MSP	Managing Successful Programmes
N/A	Not Applicable
NAO	National Audit Office (UK government body)
NPV	Net Present Value
OGC	Office of Government Commerce, part of HM Treasury
PERT	Programme Evaluation and Review Technique
PESTLE	Analysis of political, economic, social, technological, legal, environmental factors
PFI	Private Finance Initiative
PPM	Project Profile Model
PRINCE2™	The standard UK government method for project management that provides a process-based framework for setting up and controlling projects; the acronym stands for 'projects in controlled environments'
PSO	Programme or Project Support Office
RAG status	Flag that can be used to indicate status of the exposure of a risk, the status of which is denoted by colour – red, amber or green
RAGB	Flag that can be used to indicate the status of the exposure of a risk, the status of which is denoted by colour – red, amber, green or blue
ROCE	Return On Capital Employed
ROI	Return On Investment
RPA	Risk Potential Assessment
SRO	Senior Responsible Owner
SRP	Summary Risk Profile
SWOT	Analysis of strengths, weaknesses, opportunities and threats within the given situation

DEFINITIONS LIST

Accounting Officer

A public sector role. Has personal responsibility for the propriety and regularity of the finances for which he or she is answerable; for the keeping of proper accounts; for prudent and economical administration; for avoidance of waste and extravagance; and for the efficient and effective use of resources. This brings with it a responsibility for governance issues, and includes custodianship of risk management and its adoption throughout the organisation.

Audit committee

A body of independent directors who are responsible for monitoring the integrity of the financial statement of the company; the effectiveness of the company's internal audit function; and the external auditor's independence and objectivity; and the effectiveness of the audit process.

Benefits

The measurable improvement resulting from an outcome perceived as an advantage by one or more stakeholders.

Business case

The justification for an organisational activity (strategic, programme, project or operational) which typically contains costs, benefits, risks and timescales and against which continuing viability is tested.

Business change manager

The role responsible for benefits management, from identification through to realisation and ensuring the implementation and embedding of the new capabilities delivered by the projects. Typically allocated to more than one individual. Alternative title: change agent.

Business continuity management (BCM)

A holistic management process that identifies potential impacts that threaten an organisation and provides a framework for building resilience with the capability for an effective response that safeguards the interests of its key stakeholders, reputation, brand and value creating activities. The management of recovery or continuity in the event of a disaster. Also the management of the overall process through training, rehearsals and reviews, to ensure the business continuity plan stays current and up-to-date.

Business continuity plan (BCP)

A plan for the fast and efficient resumption of essential business operations by directing recovery actions of specified recovery teams.

Business risk

Failure to achieve business objectives/benefits.

Communications plan

A plan of the communications activities during the organisational activity (strategic, programme, project or operational) that will be established and maintained. Typically contains when, what, how and with whom information flows.

Contingency plan

A plan to be executed if a particular risk occurs in order to minimise the impact after the event.

Contingency planning

The process of identifying and planning appropriate responses to be taken when a risk actually occurs.

Corporate governance

The ongoing activity of maintaining a sound system of internal control by which the directors and officers of an organisation ensure that effective management systems, including financial monitoring and control systems, have been put in place to protect assets, earnings capacity and the reputation of the organisation.

CRAMM

A formalised security risk analysis and management methodology originally developed by CCTA (now part of the OGC) in collaboration with a number of private sector organisations.

Disaster recovery planning

A series of processes that focus on recovery processes, principally in response to physical disasters. This activity forms part of business continuity planning, not the totality.

Dis-benefit

Outcomes perceived as negative by one or more stakeholders. Dis-benefits are actual consequences of an activity whereas, by definition, a risk has some uncertainty about whether it will materialise.

Enhancement

A risk response for an opportunity. Enhancement of an opportunity refers to both the realisation of an opportunity and achieving additional gains over and above the opportunity.

Expected value

This is calculated by multiplying the average impact by the probability percentage.

Exploitation

A risk response for an opportunity. Exploitation refers to changing an activity's scope, suppliers or specification in order to achieve a beneficial outcome.

Gateway reviews

Independent assurance reviews that occur at key decision points within the lifecycle of a programme or project.

Horizon scanning

The systematic examination of potential threats, opportunities and likely future developments which are at the margins of current thinking and planning.

Impact

Impact is the result of a particular threat or opportunity actually occurring.

Inherent risk

The exposure arising from a specific risk before any action has been taken to manage it.

Issue

A relevant event that has happened, was not planned and requires management action. It could be a problem, query, concern, change request or risk that has occurred.

Issue actionee

A role or individual responsible for the management and control of all aspects of individual issues, including the implementation of the measures taken in respect of each issue.

Management of risk framework

Sets the context within which risks are managed, in terms of how they will be identified, assessed and controlled. It must be consistent and comprehensive, with processes that are embedded in management activities throughout the organisation.

Maturity level

A well-defined evolutionary plateau towards achieving a mature process (five levels are often cited: initial, repeatable, defined, managed and optimising).

OGC Gateway Reviews™

Independent assured reviews of major (high-risk) projects in the UK Government. They are mandatory, and occur at key decision points within the lifecycle of a project. See www.ogc.gov.uk for details.

Operational risk

Failure to achieve business/organisational objectives due to human error, system failures and inadequate procedure and controls.

Opportunity

An uncertain event that could have a favourable impact on objectives or benefits.

Outcome

The result of change, normally affecting real-world behaviour or circumstances. Outcomes are desired when a change is conceived. Outcomes are achieved as a result of the activities undertaken to effect the change.

Output

The tangible or intangible artefact produced, constructed or created as a result of a planned activity.

Probability

This is the evaluated likelihood of a particular threat or opportunity actually happening, including a consideration of the frequency with which this may arise.

Product

An input or output, whether tangible or intangible, that can be described in advance, created and tested. Also known as an output or deliverable.

Programme

A temporary, flexible organisation structure created to coordinate, direct and oversee the implementation of a set of related projects and activities in order to deliver outcomes and benefits related to the organisation's strategic objectives. A programme is likely to have a life that spans several years.

Programme risk

Risk concerned with transforming high-level strategy into new ways of working to deliver benefits to the organisation.

Project

A temporary organisation that is created for the purpose of delivering one or more business products according to a specified business case.

Project risk

Project risks are those concerned with the successful completion of the project. Typically these risks include personal, technical, cost, schedule, resource, operational support, quality and supplier issues.

Proximity (of risk)

The time factor of risk, i.e. the occurrence of risks will be due at particular times, and the severity of their impact will vary depending on when they occur.

Quality assurance

Assurance that products will be fit for purpose or meet requirements.

Realisation

A risk response for an opportunity. The realisation of opportunities ensures that potential improvements to an organisational activity are delivered.

Reduction

A risk response for a threat. Proactive actions are taken to reduce:

- The probability of the event occurring by performing some form of control, or
- The impact of the threat should it occur.

Removal

A risk response for a threat. Typically involves changing an aspect of the organisational activity, i.e. changing the scope, procurement route, supplier or sequence of activities.

Residual risk

The risk remaining after the risk response has been applied.

Retention

A risk response for a threat. A conscious and deliberate decision is taken to retain the threat, having discerned that it is more economical to do so than to attempt a risk response action. The threat should continue to be monitored to ensure that it remains tolerable.

Risk

An uncertain event or set of events that, should it occur, will have an effect on the achievement of objectives. A risk is measured by a combination of the probability of a perceived threat or opportunity occurring and the magnitude of its impact on objectives.

Risk actionee

Some actions may not be within the remit of the risk owner to control explicitly; in that situation there should be a nominated owner of the action to address the risk. He or she will need to keep the risk owner apprised of the situation.

Risk appetite

An organisation's unique attitude towards risk taking, which in turn dictates the amount of risk that it considers acceptable.

Risk cause

A description of the source of the risk, i.e. the event or situation that gives rise to the risk.

Risk committee

A body of independent directors who are responsible for reviewing the company's internal control and risk management systems.

Risk effect

A description of the impact that the risk would have on the organisational activity should the risk materialise.

Risk estimation

The estimation of probability and impact of an individual risk, taking into account predetermined standards, target risk levels, interdependencies and other relevant factors.

Risk evaluation

The process of understanding the net effect of the identified threats and opportunities on an activity when aggregated together.

Risk event

A description of the area of uncertainty in terms of the threat or the opportunity.

Risk identification

Determination of what could pose a risk; a process to describe and list sources of risk (threats and opportunities).

Risk Log

See Risk Register.

Risk Management

Systematic application of principles, approach and processes to the tasks of identifying and assessing risks, and then planning and implementing risk responses.

Risk Management Strategy

Describes the goals of applying risk management to the activity, a description of the process that will be adopted, the roles and responsibilities, risk thresholds, the timing of risk management interventions, the deliverables, the tools and techniques that will be used and reporting requirements. It may also describe how the process will be coordinated with other management activities.

Risk Management Policy

A high-level statement showing how risk management will be handled throughout the organisation.

Risk Management Process Guide

Describes the series of steps (from Identify through to Implement) and their respective associated activities, necessary to implement risk management.

Risk manager

A role or individual responsible for the implementation of risk management for each activity at each of the organisational levels.

Risk owner

A role or individual responsible for the management and control of all aspects of individual risks, including the implementation of the measures taken in respect of each risk.

Risk perception

The way in which a stakeholder views a risk, based on a set of values or concerns.

Risk potential assessment (RPA)

A standard set of high-level criteria against which the intrinsic characteristics and degree of difficulty of a proposed project are assessed. Used in the UK public sector assess the criticality of projects and so determine the level of OGC Gateway Review required.

Risk profile

Describes the types of risk faced by an organisation and its exposure to those risks.

Risk Register

A record of all identified risks relating to an initiative, including their status and history. Also called a Risk Log.

Risk response

Actions that may be taken to bring the situation to a level where the exposure to risk is acceptable to the organisation. These responses fall into one of a number of risk response categories – see below.

Risk response category

For threats, the individual risk response category can be reduction, removal, transfer, retention or share of one or more risks.

For opportunities, the individual risk response category can be realisation, enhancement or exploitation or share of one or more risks.

Risk tolerance

The threshold levels of risk exposure, which with appropriate approvals, can be exceeded, but which when exceeded, will trigger some form of response (e.g. reporting the situation to senior management for action).

Risk tolerance line

A line drawn on the Summary Risk Profile. Risks that appear above this line cannot be accepted (lived with) without referring them to a higher authority. For a project, the project manager would refer these risks to the senior responsible owner.

Senior responsible owner (SRO)

The single individual with overall responsibility for ensuring that a project or programme meets its objectives and delivers the projected benefits.

Severity of risk

The degree to which the risk could affect the situation.

Share

A risk response for a threat. Modern procurement methods commonly entail a form of risk sharing through the application of a pain/gain formula: both parties share the gain (within pre-agreed limits) if the cost is less than the cost plan; and share the pain (again within pre-agreed limits) if the cost plan is exceeded.

Sponsor

The main driving force behind a programme or project.

Sponsoring group

The main driving force behind a programme providing investment decisions and top-level endorsement of the rationale and objectives of the programme.

Stakeholder

Any individual, group or organisation that can affect, be affected by, or perceive itself to be affected by, an initiative (programme, project, activity or risk).

Statement of internal control (SIC)

A narrative statement by the board of directors of a company disclosing that there is an ongoing process for the identification and management of significant risks faced by the company.

Strategic risk

Risk concerned with where the organisation wants to go, how it plans to get there, and how it can ensure survival.

Summary Risk Profile

A simple mechanism to increase the visibility of risks. It is a graphical representation of information normally found on an existing Risk Register.

Threat

An uncertain event that could have a negative impact on objectives or benefits.

Transfer

A risk response for a threat. Whereby a third party takes on responsibility for an aspect of the threat.

Index

Index